Acting in Concert

Acting in Concert

Music, Community, and Political Action

MARK MATTERN

RUTGERS UNIVERSITY PRESS
New Brunswick, New Jersey, and London

Parts of chapter 7 are reprinted from *American Indian Culture and Research Journal*, vol. 20, no. 4, by permission of the American Indian Studies Center, UCLA. © Regents of the University of California.

Library of Congress Cataloging-in-Publication Data

Mattern, Mark, 1954–
    Acting in conert : music, community, and political action / Mark Mattern.
        p.   cm.
    Includes bibliographical references and index.
    ISBN 0-8135-2483-0 (cloth : alk. paper). — ISBN 0-8135-2484-9 (pbk. : alk. paper)
    1. Popular music—Political aspects. 2. Popular music—Social aspects. 3. Political anthropology. 4. Music and society. I. Title.
ML3470.M38   1998
306.2—dc21
                                            97-21868
                                          CIP
                                          MN

British Cataloging-in-Publication information available

Manufactured in the United States of America

Contents

Acknowledgments

THE EMPIRICAL RESEARCH for this book hardly felt like a chore. I traveled to interesting places, interviewed fascinating people (some of whom became good friends), listened to good music, and jammed with talented musicians. But turning the research into a book proved less pleasant and more challenging, and I would never have finished without the support of many individuals and organizations. Each contributor shares the credit for whatever merits this book may possess but shoulders none of the burden for its flaws.

In Chile, I thank Eliana Andaur, Maritza Andaur, Carlos Castillo, Teresa Castillo, Mari Carmen Cortéz, José Flores, Gloria Rojas, and Eugenia Neves for their insights about popular music and for their friendship. I also thank Eduardo Carrasco, Carlos Catalán, Rene Largo Farías, Ricardo García, Álvaro Godoy, Carlos Pino, María de la Luz Silva, and Bernardo Subercaseaux for their generous assistance. For helping me enter more deeply into the world of Cajun and zydeco music, I thank Barry Ancelet, Lawrence Ardoin, Pete Bergeron, Joe Bodi, Carl Brasseaux, Earline Broussard, Glenn Conrad, Don Cravins, Pat Cravins, Takuna Maulana El Shabazz, Ruth Foote, Wilbert Guillory, Rebecca Henry, Katrinna Huggs, Todd Mouton, Wayne Parent, Pat Rickels, and Herbert Wiltz. For sharing their insights about powwows, I thank Julie Beaulieu, Wayne Carson, Darwin Cook, Robert Danforth, Ruth Denny, John Kearney, Bruce Meyers, Cornel Pewewardy, and Sammy Watso.

My field research was supported by grants from the MacArthur Foundation, the University of Minnesota's Conflict and Change Center, and Chapman University. I especially thank Tom Fiutak, associate director of the Conflict and Change Center, for his friendship and patient support.

I benefited from the support and advice given to me as a graduate student at the University of Minnesota groping my way through a dissertation project. In particular, Terence Ball, Harry Boyte, Mary Dietz, Lisa Disch, James Farr, Larry May, Susan McClary, and Kathryn Sikkink deserve my hearty thanks for their advice and support. They should be commended for allowing, even encouraging, a political theorist to write a dissertation on music—at best, a marginal topic in political science. I especially owe a large debt of gratitude to Mary Dietz for her intellectual guidance and personal support. I also thank Ed Portis at Texas A&M for his careful reading of the manuscript and his helpful suggestions for improving it.

I am fortunate to work among talented and supportive colleagues at Chapman University who indirectly supported this project. I especially thank my fellow political scientists Art Blaser, Fred Smoller, Ron Steiner, and Don Will. A more collegial department is hard to imagine. Special thanks are also due to Roberta Lessor and Lee Estes, past and current chairs of the Chapman University Social Sciences Division, for their efforts to support junior faculty and lead us toward the promised land of tenure. I thank Finn Wilhelmsen for his insightful comments and helpful suggestions for improving the manuscript and thank the other members of the Social Sciences Division for creating a personal and professional environment that encourages excellence.

Many thanks are due to Martha Heller at Rutgers University Press for helping shape the manuscript both intellectually and aesthetically. Her insights, suggestions, enthusiasm, and humor made working with the press a pleasure.

I was tempted when writing this book to wrestle with it during every spare moment. Fortunately, my family offered more interesting and satisfying temptations. I thank my wife, Katherine Kratz, for helping make life away from work joyful and stimulating and for her emotional support and intellectual comradeship. I thank my son, Leon Kratz, for luring me away from work to dance, build forts, and play hide-and-seek. Without the two of them anchoring my life, I would accomplish little of value or significance. To them, I dedicate this work.

Acting in Concert

Introduction

JULY 1989. On Paseo Ahumado, a crowded pedestrian street in downtown Santiago, Chile, twenty men work on the side of a building, several stories above the ground. A group of four musicians begins to play
below them, and a small crowd of about thirty people quickly gathers.
After a brief introduction extolling the virtues of Santiago's working-
class population and decrying its many problems, the musicians begin
a song called "Hacen falta muchas cosas para conseguir la paz" [there
remains much to do in order to achieve peace], which tells how the
people must work against injustice with the tools that they have, including songs and guitars.

> In my country there will be no peace,
> so long as there is exploitation
> of men by men, creating inequality.
> Nothing can be achieved without revolution.
> The singer is always ready to defend the country,
> with the voice and the guitar against rifles and guns.

The construction workers stop to listen, and the musicians encourage the crowd to clap and sing along. But they ask everyone to avoid
blocking the sidewalk to reduce the likelihood that the military, who
seized power in 1973 in a bloody coup and whose presence in 1989 remains ubiquitous, will intervene. One of the musicians introduces the

next song and dedicates it to Agosto Pinochet, architect of the coup
and leader of the military junta, and to Pinochet's bicycle program,
which is aimed at getting people to use bicycles rather than cars to ease
the smog. Following each verse, the crowd joins in the refrain:

> He's going to fall.
> The people are certain, he is sure to fall.
> Chile doesn't give up, that's the popular saying.

Members of the crowd sing loudly and without hesitation, indicating that they are familiar with the song. Despite the earnestness of the
music, everyone smiles and laughs, for the song involves a triple pun.
On the one hand, the singers jokingly imply that the construction workers above are going to fall, a point that they emphasize with shouts and
gestures. Because the musicians have already made it clear in their initial greeting that they view themselves as allies of the workers, no of-
fense is taken. Instead, the construction workers laugh and shout
encouragement. At the same time, the singers pointedly suggest that
Pinochet is going to fall from power *and* that he will fall off his bicycle.
After playing two more songs, the musicians move away, and the crowd
disperses.

The musicians' act of rebellion signals the survival of a political
community of Chileans committed to redemocratization while helping
maintain it in existence. Their songs help reinforce and re-create the
identifying commitments of this political community. In a context of
ongoing military repression, these guerilla musicians play an oppositional, destabilizing role in the streets of Santiago. They help
marginalized Chileans reopen political spaces violently closed by the
military junta and act politically within them.

Six o'clock in the evening on a Friday in October 1993. The main
street of downtown Lafayette, Louisiana, is empty of cars, which have
been replaced by a growing throng of women, men, and children con-
suming beer, soft drinks, and grilled hamburgers purchased from the vendors lining the street. A large stage stands in the middle of the central
intersection. On it plays a Cajun band—accordionist, fiddler, guitarist,
bassist, and drummer. The musicians announce that their next song will
be the traditional waltz "Jolie blonde." For most of the dancers who fill

the intersection and spill into surrounding streets, the tune needs no introduction; like most people in southwest Louisiana, they could identify it within seconds, tell any outsider that it is a favorite traditional Cajun waltz, and probably recite its history as well. The accordionist begins playing, the rest of the band joins in, and the dancers start waltzing. The next dance is a two-step, followed by a jitterbug. Even children appear on the "dance floor," and everyone seems to know the steps. Throughout the evening, the famous Cajun *joie de vivre* remains in ample supply.

Although there are no speeches, no guest appearances, and no appeals made to the crowd, this is a party with a purpose. The Lafayette Chamber of Commerce created this weekly event, Downtown Alive!, to promote the vitality of downtown Lafayette by keeping office workers there after working hours and luring in tourists to patronize downtown bars and restaurants. Participants in this and many other events like it celebrate Cajun culture while affirming their membership in an extensive community of Cajuns and supporters committed to cultural and economic revitalization in southwest Louisiana. Because musicians initiated a cultural revival in the 1960s, they are called upon frequently to organize the community and drive collaborative efforts to solve community problems, especially economic marginalization, ethnic stigma, and cultural survival.

SHORTLY AFTER DUSK on July 9, 1993. The Prairie Island Dakota traditional powwow, held outdoors under the stars, is in full swing. It is a beautiful Minnesota evening, with only an occasional tormenting mosquito. The night air, filled with the swirling scent of fried bread and Indian tacos, tobacco and sage, is still cooling after a hot day. Surrounded by trees and bleachers, food and craft vendors, dancers and spectators, and, beyond them, cars, trucks, tents, teepees, and recreational vehicles, the circular powwow arena lies within easy shouting distance of the tribe's fancy new casino. Outside the arena, adults relax and chat, watch the dancers, and visit with old and new friends. Children and youths run, play, and shout.

Inside the dance arena, the popular Black Lodge Singers perform an intertribal song. Adults, youths, and children in various outfits dance slowly around the circle. The singers are talented, the dancing skilled and enthusiastic. Drum groups ring the perimeter of the arena, waiting their turn to play and sing. As the Black Lodge Singers near the end of the song, one of the dancers blows a carved whistle. The singers recognize the cue and respond by taking another pass through the song. Again, as they near the conclusion of the song, a dancer blows a whistle; and, again, the singers return to the beginning of the song. As they play, a tribal elder walks slowly to the emcee's stand, takes the microphone, and, when the song finally ends, begins speaking to the dancers and the crowd. He admonishes his listeners, reminding them that the carved whistle carries spiritual significance. It should, he tells them, be retained for its proper spiritual use in rituals and ceremonies. Do not use the whistle, he says, to goad favored singers. This diminishes its spiritual value. When he finishes, he hands the microphone back to the emcee and leaves the stand. The next drum group begins playing, and the dancers respond.

By questioning the secular use of the carved whistle, the elder has reminded his listeners of the whistle's spiritual significance for the Dakota people. He has challenged others to consider their beliefs and the significance of their actions in light of their beliefs. In doing so, he transforms the powwow arena into a public space for debate and deliberation about secular versus spiritual uses of the carved whistle and, more broadly, about the relative weight in Indian life of secular versus spiritual concerns.

Indians disagree about many issues. Their differences are as pronounced as their similarities, and the powwow is a place where these differences can be negotiated. At the same time, the powwow arena is a public space where the practices that identify members of different tribes *as* tribal and American Indians can be reproduced, re-created, and maintained, thus ensuring a better chance of survival.

EACH VIGNETTE ILLUSTRATES a distinctly different form of acting in concert, which is a metaphor for community-based political action through music.[1] In this book, I address the extent to which Chileans, Cajuns, and American Indians in Minnesota and western Wisconsin have used popular music as a means of defining and maintaining diverse communities as well as a way of promoting distinct forms of collective political action. *Community* represents a theoretical and practical means through which disparate individuals come to recognize and act upon common concerns and interests, negotiate differences, and assert themselves in public arenas. The communities that musicians have helped to form and sustain provide the social basis for political action that would be difficult or impossible among individuals who are not tied together in this way.

There are many empirical examples of explicit political uses of music, ranging from Sting's environmental statements, to large fund- and consciousness-raising concerts, such as FarmAid, to the political commentary in rap music. But the potential political significance of music extends well beyond these explicit uses to include, for example, its impact on human identity and capacity, its role in defining or destroying communities, and its part in cultural revitalization and self-determination. Researchers in many academic disciplines have produced an extensive literature documenting these connections between politics and music. Most researchers have focused on highly commercialized, mass-based forms of music such as rock and pop music, but others have studied more marginal forms of popular music such as ethnic, world-beat, and folk. Because I have chosen to explore the relationship among the music, community, and political practices of relatively marginalized and distinct groups of people, I fit more readily into the latter category. I make no attempt, however, to address political music or the politics of music comprehensively. Such an undertaking would be difficult, perhaps impossible, given the astonishing variety of ways in which music and politics are intertwined. Instead, I focus on the question of acting in concert.

Oddly, political scientists and political theorists have made few contributions to the literature of music and politics and have shown little interest in exploring the political dimensions of music or other forms of popular culture.[2] The absence from this field of political theorists and political scientists at least raises the suspicion that the concerns of political scientists and theorists are underrepresented in the literature. This proves to be especially true in three ways. First, when the concept of community appears (as it does infrequently) in the existing literature of music, it is typically formulated in organic, apolitical terms that erase disagreement and difference, and it is justified on psychological grounds as a tonic for alienation and isolation rather than on political grounds as a social basis for collective political action. Second, the concept of power is often either absent or conceived in limited ways to mean, for example, perceptions of power rather than actual power that can enable democratic changes in people's lives. Third, political action is frequently reduced to one form involving struggle, opposition, and resistance. Although this is a legitimate form of political action, it is not the only, nor necessarily the best, available form. In each of these three areas, the unique perspective of a political theorist might shed additional light on the subject.

I pose several questions in this book. For example, under what circumstances does popular music contribute to the formation and maintenance of community? To what degree does popular music help reconcile the tension between diversity and community or between multiple differences and our need to recognize and act on common interests? What kinds of alternative political arenas does popular music open? Which forms of acting in concert can be identified? To what degree does popular music enable people to make real democratic changes in their lives? What contribution does music make to the vitality of communal and public life and to democratic life in general?

I argue that popular music can be the social glue for creating and maintaining diverse communities; that these communities support several distinct forms of collective political action including intracommunal disagreement and debate as well as assertion in external public arenas; and that music can increase the capacity, or power, of relatively marginalized people to choose and determine their own fate. While these are common themes of this book, their particular expression varies according to historical and cultural context. My three case studies—Chilean, Cajun, and American Indian popular music—have allowed me to explore different expressions of these themes in varying historical and cultural contexts.

What Lies Ahead?

There are many different formulations of community and many different justifications for it. In the first part of chapter 1, I explain and formulate the concept of community in democratic, political terms that are consistent with diversity and that support widespread citizen involvement in public life. In the second part, I link community to popular music by arguing that music is both an expression and, potentially, a determinant of diverse communities and that it can serve as a bridge between different people and communities by offering an accessible form of communication across cultural boundaries.

Political action is also at the core of acting in concert. While political theorists identify distinctly different kinds of political action, popular music researchers often focus exclusively on one form that emphasizes the language and practices of struggle, resistance, and opposition. In the first part of chapter 2, I broaden the potential links between popular music and political action by developing three distinct forms of acting in concert, each representing a particular form of community-based political action. I call these forms *deliberative*, *pragmatic*, and *confrontational*.

Of course, political action through music may or may not result in democratic change. The result depends in part on power—on the variable capacity of different individuals and groups to critically define and achieve their goals. Power is central to an understanding of the relative success or failure of acting in concert to produce desired changes in a social and political environment. In the second part of chapter 2, I discuss power in terms developed by political theorists in order to deepen and sharpen its application to popular culture; and I connect power in several ways to popular music. I emphasize power to avoid celebrating acting in concert apart from its actual outcomes, which inevitably romanticizes it.

Chapters 3 through 7 include the results of my empirical research on Chilean popular music, Cajun music, and American Indian pow-wow music in Minnesota and western Wisconsin. I use these concrete cases to sharpen, illuminate, deepen, and focus the insights of the preceding theoretical chapters. In each case study, I examine music in terms of its contribution to the formation and maintenance of community, the political action that it enables, and the concrete outcomes of acting in concert. These cases vividly illustrate the theme of acting in concert—of community-based political action through music—but in significantly different ways. Their similarities allow me to link them thematically, while their differences allow me to address interesting questions raised by their contrasts. One point of contrast, for example, is the degree to which each is overtly political. While most of Chilean popular music is explicitly political in intent and orientation, allowing me to probe connections between popular music and movement-based and institutionalized politics, Cajun music is less explicitly political, requiring instead a more challenging and profound argument about the politics of community-based music. Powwow music is interesting, among other reasons, because American Indians disagree about its political significance. Some use powwow music for explicit political ends, while others take pains to disconnect the music from politics altogether, arguing that politics disrupts the music's essentially spiritual dimension. Nevertheless, although each case differs considerably from the others, similar themes and issues also arise.

I have included a brief history with each case in order to establish a social, cultural, and political context and to demonstrate the concrete relation between music and community. Each case also includes a discussion of the extent to which music is responsible for the formation and maintenance of an explicitly political community that is capable of recognizing and acting on common interests and that shares the means and commitment to debate differences and disagreements. In each case various forms of acting in concert are addressed and their political significance assessed. Finally, each case includes a discussion of power, framed primarily in terms of the contribution that music makes to political capacity.

	Popular Music
Chapter 1	and Community

WHAT IS COMMUNITY? How is it tied to popular music? These two questions, central to an understanding of acting in concert, are addressed in this chapter. Although the term *community* appears frequently in popular and academic literature, there is little agreement about what exactly it means. Instead, "an almost bewildering variety of conceptions of community" can be found in contemporary American intellectual life (Fowler 1991, x).

These different conceptions of community often appear to have little in common. What they do have in common is commonality. The similarity between the words *common* and *commonality* is not coincidental. People live in a community by virtue of the things that they hold in common. Nevertheless, the mere presence of commonality does not necessarily indicate a community. For example, a common consumption of rap music does not automatically call a community into being.

At what point, then, does common become community? The question is difficult to answer in the abstract. Community is an open, contested concept whose definitive characteristics cannot simply be stipulated.[1] Communities are defined by a set of common characteristics, and the identity of a particular community is defined by the specific character of its commonalities. For example, communities are defined by specific common traits of political identity, political commitment, memory, history, tradition, and culture; by variations in their degree of openness; and in their size and scope. In my exploration of acting in concert, I am interested in a specifically democratic conception of community that is consistent with diversity, supports collective political action and a strong form of democracy, and potentially encompasses extensive populations and geographical regions as well as local settings.[2]

Democratic Community

In most populations, we must begin from the fact of diversity—multiple differences of gender, class, race, sexual orientation, ethnicity, culture, political interest, and political commitment.[3] Difference, however, is not absolute; common and different coexist in most social environments. People in very disparate circumstances face similar challenges and life experiences that motivate similar, if not identical, intellectual and emotional responses. Moreover, many important social and political issues today span not only local, regional, and national differences but global as well. In other words, both common and incompatible interests exist in most political contexts at local, national, and international levels.

Although diversity does not preclude commonalities of interest and identity, it does ensure that some interests are incompatible. A political conception of community recognizes the probability within a diverse population of divergent interests, the disagreement and conflict that result from these divergences, and the consequent need to negotiate and accommodate differences. How these differences are handled partly determines the democratic or undemocratic character of the community. At a minimum, parochial interests and self-interests cannot simply be dismissed as illegitimate concerns in public life.

Some conceptions of community hold that members must be altruistic. If this means a one-sided attention to the common good and denial of self-interest, then it is inappropriate and unnecessary in a diverse political community. History suggests that such a conception demands too much of citizens and is unrealistic. More important, it requires that individual interests be ignored or devalued in favor of communal interests. The potential for incursions on individual freedom loom large in such a scenario. On the other hand, one important skill of community members is an ability and willingness to weigh self-interests in light of common and public interests.

Although diversity is compatible with community, it nevertheless poses potentially daunting challenges for collective political action. How do citizens in social environments that combine both compatible and incompatible interests work out their differences peacefully and productively in a way that avoids social breakdown and retains the ability to recognize and act upon shared concerns? Community offers a theoretical and practical response. While community is justified on various grounds, its principle political justification is this need for collective political action.[4] A political conception of community links community to collective action by providing a framework for recognizing and acting upon shared interests and for negotiating and contesting divergent interests. Community is here conceived of as a social basis for political action but not as political action per se. It is an "overlapping and intermediate realm between personal and public environments" (Boyte 1992, 8). The actual work of politics builds upon, but is not the same as, communal life.

The key challenge lies in finding or creating some semblance of unity in diversity that, however temporary, uneven, and slight, enables individuals to engage in collective political action to address shared interests and to negotiate divergent ones. Although community is partly constituted by diversity, it also helps avoid a situation in which diversity produces social disintegration and failure to act on pressing problems and concerns. Without overstating the possibility, we can aspire to seek sufficient common ground to support a vigorous public life in which citizens participate in multiple forms of political action aimed at peaceful coexistence and addressing shared concerns. One modern problem is a failure to find or create this common ground amid multiple differences, leaving us with a politics of polarization and competition among unequal interest groups that often have no means of coherently addressing issues that span competing interests. Democratic community represents one potential response.

Another characteristic of community, its democratic or undemocratic nature, is revealed in the defining commitments and common political identity of its members. The most fundamental commitment within a specifically democratic community is to shared democratic values and principles, without which democratic community is impossible. Here I refer to basic democratic ends and the means for attaining them but not necessarily to any single conception of a common good that might prove hostile to individual differences. Democratic community cannot privilege a single vision of the good life because doing so would overwhelm moral pluralism and individual rights.[5]

Freedom and equality are basic principles of a democratic community. It is essential, however, to understand them in a way that supports a rich democratic life and is inconsistent with modern undemocratic elements. They must be understood in strong, or radical, democratic terms that emphasize effective freedom and real, as opposed to merely formal or legal, political equality. Effective freedom is socially supported freedom that entails actual choices and options, not simply the absence of visible impediments. This requires attention not only to "cramping and thwarting obstacles" but also to a positive "capacity to vary plans, to change the course of action," and an "ability to carry out plans" (Dewey 1922, 278–79).[6] In other words, it requires attention to power as both a limiting and enabling factor in human volition and action.

One myth of contemporary U.S. politics is that, because the Constitution guarantees freedom to each citizen equally, freedom is therefore distributed equally in practice. According to this view, each citizen is as free as another to make choices and act on them. But that conception is patently false. American citizens experience wide disparities in their ability to make choices and act upon them, depending, for example, on circumstances of their birth, the color of their skin, their economic status, and their gender.

Real political equality is equality in which each citizen's voice carries equal weight. A second myth of contemporary politics is that political equality already exists in the United States because each citizen is entitled to one vote, and only one. In practice, there are wide variations in political power based on differences such as race, gender, ethnicity, and, especially, economic status. At a minimum, real political equality requires a greater degree of economic equality than is currently the case or more effective assurances that economic power will not translate into political power. Equality means that the needs and interests of privileged individuals and groups must not take systematic precedence over those of more marginalized individuals and groups.

Without a commitment to these stronger versions of freedom and equality, democracy will remain incomplete, falling well short of its ideals. Average citizens will continue to be marginalized by elites with exceptional economic and political power, a situation that already fuels apathy and cynicism. This, in turn, will continue to undermine the widespread, effective participation of average citizens. Thus, effective freedom and real political equality are both the ends and means of democratic community: ends because they partly embody the conditions of an enriching, satisfying, creative life for individuals within a democratic community; means because they help enable full participation in communal life.

The common political identity of community members also defines the democratic or undemocratic nature of the community. In a democratic community, this common identity has two central dimensions: first, identification with the democratic values and principles that I have just discussed; second, a set of civic skills and dispositions. Identification with democratic values and principles is necessary to ensure continued commitment to, and revitalization of, the central democratic processes and institutions of democratic life. Citizens identify with their community, its members, and its defining characteristics. They see themselves as members of a common political body and recognize the importance of its core values and principles. This lends an element of cohesiveness and coherence to an otherwise heterogeneous population and ensures the potency of commitments to defining traits of the community.[7]

Civic skills and dispositions are necessary for the responsible and effective participation of average citizens. What are these skills and dispositions? Contemporary communitarians emphasize a shared political identity that includes a sense of personal and civic responsibility, a common appreciation of our own and others' rights, mutual possession of skills of self-government and habits of governing ourselves, and mutual willingness to serve others as well as ourselves.[8] Although each element is important, one particular skill of self-government must be emphasized in a community whose members are diverse and heterogeneous: the ability to handle the demands of diversity, to recognize and cope with it. Members of a democratic community must be willing and able to weigh self-interests in light of common and public interests; to think critically about the pursuit of individual and common ends; and to listen, discuss, and deliberate with people unlike themselves. These are necessary in order to avoid undemocratic domination by parochial interests, to avoid the imposition of single or undemocratic conceptions of a common good, and to sustain a robust political life marked by widespread citizen participation.

Although local communities are important for solving local problems and nurturing citizenship skills, they cannot be taken as the only, or even the main, site of public life. Given our need to address a multitude of pressing problems spanning local communities, citizens must acquire the dispositions and skills for addressing public affairs in larger arenas. If community is to serve usefully in today's world, it must be capable of encompassing more extensive domains. Some critics allege that community is only possible in local neighborhood settings. Implicitly or explicitly, these critics argue that community requires intimate, face-to-face relations to sustain the common bonds of community. Even some defenders of community make this claim.[9] But this view is a mistake that hinges on an implicit assumption about the nature of the communication that brings community into being and sustains it.

I have already noted the similarity between *common* and *community*. *Communication* bears the same similarity. It is through communication that people develop the commonalities of community. Most political theorists mistakenly reduce communication to speech, while some theorists and critics of community mistakenly reduce the term even further to speech among neighbors. An emphasis on communication in multiple forms—including popular music—as a way of "making common" enables us to sidestep the objection raised by these critics that community requires face-to-face relations and is thus unworkable in an extended republic. Even local community need not rely entirely on direct personal interactions, given the many forms of communication possible today: not only traditional print and broadcast media such as newspapers and network television but also burgeoning alternative forms such as electronic mail, the Internet, and a cable television market tied closely to distinct neighborhoods, communities, and cities.

If community does not require local, face-to-face, personal contact, it nevertheless is always connected to particular times and places because people's identity is formed in actual concrete interactions with specific social and cultural environments at specific historical times. It would thus be impossible to imagine a human disconnected from a particular time and place and impossible to imagine a community formed by humans that is not rooted in a concrete social and historical context. Yet this same formulation allows us to imagine a community that is not *limited* to one time and place. Communication in multiple forms opens the possibility of sharing experience both temporally and spatially and therefore building communities that span generations and geographical regions. This is a crucial point in evaluating the feasibility of extensive and heterogeneous communities.

Popular Music and Community

John Dewey wrote:

> Works of art that are not remote from common life, that are widely enjoyed in a community, are signs of a unified collective life. But they are also marvelous aids in the creation of such a life. The remaking of the material of experience in the act of expression is not an isolated event confined to the artist and to a person here and there who happens to enjoy the work. In the degree in which art exercises its office, it is also a remaking of the experience of the community in the direction of greater order and unity. (Dewey 1934, 81)

Like Dewey, I believe that art forms such as music can be both "signs" and "marvelous aids in the creation of" community.[10] As a sign of community, music reveals constituent elements such as beliefs, assumptions, and commitments that define the character and shape of the community. As a "marvelous aid," or determinant, music provides a form of communication through which the commonalities of community are created and discovered. In order to make this argument persuasive, we must recognize the social nature of music and appreciate its significance.

The text of popular music—its structure, sound, and lyrical content—is surely an important dimension to address in considering its politics. The text is rich with social meaning and can be analyzed in terms of what it reveals about a social context. But the politics of popular music are not limited to this text. Popular music operates within a social context that also includes the people and sites directly and indirectly involved in its production, consumption, and use. In other words, the political work of a piece of music also occurs in the multiple ways that people use it and in the ways that it circulates in a context. The wider context of reception and use defines a communicative arena in which meanings are created, shared, negotiated, and changed and in which various individuals and groups appropriate music for different ends.

This communicative arena is not limited to direct musical experience. Popular music creates a communicative arena that extends beyond music per se to include related social practices. For example, the communal and political significance of 1960s rock music is surely tied to the concrete musical product of the Beatles, Bob Dylan, Jimi Hendrix, and Janis Joplin. Listeners responded to the musical sounds and lyrical messages, weaving them into their everyday lives. Although the text was often heavily weighted with political messages, the social and political significance of the music was not limited to the songs themselves. The music helped create and sustain a countercultural and political movement associated with drug experimentation, generational rebellion, and opposition to the Vietnam War. It helped create various communicative arenas, ranging from huge concerts such as Woodstock, to informal gatherings in homes, to dance halls in high schools and colleges—all of them nurturing the movement and giving it room in which to develop. The music opened social and public spaces for the communicative interactions that are necessary for the sharing of meaning and the creation of commonalities of identity and orientation. In addition to music, these interactions included everyday conversation, affective interplay and expression, and dance—social practices that defined spaces in which youth and others could identify each other as members of a group with shared characteristics.

A discussion of the communal role of music must also rest on solid social psychological foundations that begin with the recognition that individual identity is partly formed through interaction with a social environment. Human identity is created through meaningful interactions with a social world at the same time that humans transform their world. An individual musician's character and personality is thus tied to his or her history of social experiences. Prior experiences are embodied in the present in the form of memories and meanings that are recovered and given new life in an act of musical expression. They become the means through which the musician perceives and creatively refashions the world—the "nutriment" for creative expression (Dewey 1934, 89). Each work of music recaptures and re-creates past experience, refashioning it according to present creative and practical interests and goals.

Several implications about community emerge from this social account of music. First, emphasizing the common and social determinants of music leaves ample room to theorize its communicative capacity. If music embodies common memories and meanings, then it is tied to public and objective social circumstances—to the shared experiences of people in an objective social and physical environment. The messages of music are thus publicly accessible, not merely elements of the musician's subjective and private world. This public, common quality gives music its communicative capacity, which, in turn, may support the development of community by enabling the sharing of experience.

This idea is most evident in musical lyrics, which readily express memories, histories, emotions, political ideologies, and ideas. Music, however, communicates through sound as well. Most Western listeners know how to move their bodies in time to the rhythm of Eric Clapton's "After Midnight" and most recognize sadness and mourning in the downward-bending notes of an Andean flute played in a minor key. Moreover, music provides a communicative medium that is not simply an alternative way to say the same things that humans say through speech. Music, like other art forms, can express meanings that are not accessible through words or express them in ways that give listeners more immediate access to emotions and ideas.

Unlike some other art forms, however, music is directly physical. Listeners experience music with their bodies as sound waves.[11] This physicality allows musicians to turn their moods and emotions into sounds that listeners directly share, without recourse to language, in a way that produces immediate quality of experience. Such sharing can occur at both large-scale events and more intimate settings. In both places, performers and audience members communicate with each other in a variety of ways, including singing, dancing, clapping, and swaying. In short, while the lyrical content of music more clearly communicates ideas, the physical and affective dimensions of music lend it potency as a form of communication.

A second implication of a social account of music is that music serves as a record of a civilization or community. If music captures human experience and renders it meaningful for contemporary audiences, then it is a legitimate window into the identity and history of a people. Both musical form (style) and substance (messages, content) are saturated with meanings derived from past experiences. Although we can never experience the music of another people in the same way that the people themselves do or did, we can nevertheless learn much about them from their music. Some contemporary musicologists deny this view, insisting that the meaning of music is strictly formal and structural, residing only in the relationships between sounds and wholly understandable apart from its historical and cultural context. My arguments point toward the view held by other researchers, who believe that music is deeply scored with meanings derived from historical and cultural context.[12]

A third implication of emphasizing the social determinants of music is that the experiences and memories expressed in a piece of music are not those of an isolated individual. Presumably, the musician has had many of the experiences common to others and has absorbed some of that common meaning. For example, contemporary rap music expresses the experiences not only of individual rappers but also of other black Americans who have lived in similar circumstances and places. Listening to an artist's rap, others recognize themselves and their own experiences. For many people, this is what gives rap its potency and appeal: listeners recognize their own experiences, and the meaning that they derive from those experiences, in the music. Tricia Rose (1994, 146) integrates this insight into her analysis of black women rappers, arguing that they "interpret and articulate the fears, pleasures, and promises of young black women whose voices have been relegated to the margins of public discourse." Andean folk music frequently expresses pain—for good reason, originating as it does in the often difficult lives of Andean Indians. The same can be said of African-American blues. Much traditional Irish music emphasizes the theme of leaving, reflecting the experience of living in a country that has long exported large numbers of its people. Theme is revealed in musical form as well as lyrical content. Blues musicians bend their notes freely to imitate a crying voice, as do Andean musicians playing their bamboo flutes. The instruments themselves may also reflect communal experience. For example, the Andean charango, an adaptation of the Spanish guitar, reflects the collision of Inca and European cultures.

As different people identify with a particular kind of music, they internalize some of its meaning, and it becomes part of their identity. By expressing common experiences, music helps create and solidify a fund of shared memories and a sense of "who we are." Andeans recognize the charango as distinctively theirs, and many African Americans identify with the sentiments expressed in the blues. The process is reflexive: the music expresses common experiences and, by playing and listening to it, people reexperience its sentiments and forms, which reflects back on the identity of the participants. This, in turn, may contribute to the development of community as individuals acquire and maintain an awareness of common experiences, memories, beliefs, and commitments. If the musician succeeds in integrating common experiences into a piece of music and making it comprehensible to others, he or she clarifies and reinforces the meaning of group life, bringing it into focus. The musician helps the audience recognize a relatedness that may not have existed before.

Of course, any assertion about the meaning of group life can be challenged by others. If we take diversity seriously, we should expect disagreements and conflicts within community life about its identity and commitments. The life of a diverse community is partly defined by these disagreements and conflicts, which are elements constitutive of politics. Thus, we should expect disagreements about which musical expression best represents the experiences of a given community. We should also expect that different and contradictory musical expressions might legitimately represent the varied experiences of a given individual or group. For example, gangsta rap—the strand of rap that often emphasizes anger, violence, and misogyny—accurately portrays the life experiences of some black Americans but not others. It should not be taken as paradigmatic of all black American experience, although it sometimes is, especially by uninformed listeners. Moreover, musicians may intentionally misrepresent their own experiences and those of others, sometimes resulting in unfortunate outcomes. Gangsta rappers have been accused of exaggerating some of their themes or inventing experiences in order to sell more records. One outcome of incorrectly assuming the paradigmatic status of gangsta rap and of its sometimes misleading or exaggerated themes is that white, suburban teenagers, who represent one of gangsta rap's largest groups of consumers, may internalize inaccurate understandings and beliefs about African Americans.

This potential misunderstanding is compounded by problems of interpretation and limitations on communicative capacity. People perceive different messages in music, none of which the musician may have intended. If there is room in a piece of music for interpretation, then people will disagree about its meaning. Consequently, the same piece can be appropriated for different, sometimes contradictory, uses within and between communities. For example, Simon Frith (1984) and David James (1989) both point out that rock musicians and groups such as the Rolling Stones, the Grateful Dead, and Jimi Hendrix were sources of solidarity and enthusiasm for both the antiwar movement and the American soldiers in Vietnam. Soldiers attributed meaning to "2000 Light Years From Home" (Rolling Stones), "We Gotta Get Out of This Place" (the Animals), "Green, Green Grass of Home" (Porter Wagoner), and "Leaving on a Jet Plane" (Peter, Paul, and Mary) that the authors probably did not intend.[13] Even within a particular community, the ability of a work of music to communicate common meanings to different individuals may be limited. This communicative challenge is magnified for relations between different communities. For example, can European Americans really appreciate and understand Macedonian or Persian folk music? Marked by strange harmonies, rhythms, and chord progressions, both appear strange and jarring to the uninitiated ear. Superficial exposure may increase alienation rather than motivate the mutual understanding and respect that underlies community.

Moreover, people are not necessarily interested in making an accurate interpretation of a work of music. Like other forms of art, music is frequently appropriated selectively for political ends. For example, political actors can take advantage of the disagreements within different communities about claims of authenticity, selectively choosing one voice and calling it paradigmatic. When 1992 presidential candidate Bill Clinton, with the collusion of the mainstream media, emphasized the violent messages of Sister Souljah and Ice-T and the misogyny of 2

Live Crew, he gave millions of white listeners and readers the false impression that rap music is generically violent and misogynistic. This has led to large-scale denunciations of rap music and may have fanned racism by serving as a rationale for blanket criticism of the African-American communities to which rap is tied. One unfortunate outcome may be that rap music has further separated black from white communities rather than serving as a window of understanding between them.[14]

Popular Music, Community, and Diversity

In addition to creating and reinforcing commonalities among different people, music also creates and reinforces differences. This occurs, first, between two or more distinct communities. The same process that builds and sustains commonalities of identity and commitment also draws fluid boundaries demarcating one people from another. I have noted that human experience occurs in the context of a concrete social and physical environment and that human identity is tied to the interaction between humans and this environment. Presumably, the environment varies according to cultural and historical settings, and so, too, must the character and quality of experience. Different experiences produce a different universe of memories and meanings and, ultimately, of identity. These differences are expressed in many ways, including musically, and the expressions reinforce and re-create the identity of individuals and groups tied to concrete social and physical conditions. Therefore, music maintains the differences between different groups even as it solidifies a common identity within them. In other words, the Irish are Irish in part because of the distinctiveness of their musical expression. The way they express themselves musically helps mark them off as a distinctive people. Their music contributes to a universe of shared meanings, memories, and self-understandings that differs from the universe of other groups.

Second, music creates and reinforces differences within a particular community, and exposure to different forms of music may differentiate experience and identity within it. Despite the common characteristics that make it distinctive, Irish music takes many different forms, ranging from traditional, to rock, to punk. Exposure to these various forms

allows for different forms of experience and hence differences of identity among listeners.

These conclusions must be qualified in an era of mass communication. Today, people in widely different social and cultural environments
experience similar or identical musical forms, especially pop and rock
music originating in the United States and Great Britain. As a result,
exposure to music may homogenize rather than differentiate human experience and identity. Yet musical production and consumption remains
highly differentiated in most parts of the world. In the United States,
for example, ethnic, world-beat, and folk musics flourish alongside the
rock, rap, and country that dominate radio and television. Moreover,
competing sounds and messages are found within each of the dominant
forms. None of them represents a monolithic, homogeneous collection
of sounds or messages; all are marked by various strains, influences, and
themes that preserve the potential for differentiation of experience and
identity.

Music also may serve critical and visionary roles in making communities more open and tolerant to the experiences of others, helping
members see themselves in a new light and expanding the horizons of
the community.[15] If music communicates meanings derived from the
past and present everyday lives of a people, then each work of music
embodies assumptions and beliefs that people hold about themselves
and their lives. If the musician has taken elements from experience and
selectively reconfigured them, community members are challenged to
view their lives in new ways. The work forces a reconsideration of accepted and sanctioned beliefs, assumptions, and practices, allowing
people to see more clearly and critically. Thus, music can make communities more open to differences by undermining the preconceptions
and unconscious assumptions that sometimes underlie prejudice and
intolerance. It increases the possibility of mutual recognition and respect of differences and encourages greater modesty in asserting universal moral and political ends and judgments that are hostile to
differences.

Music may also help people see worlds that they did not know existed. Like other art forms, it is a vehicle for communicating with other
people from other communities. If music expresses the experiences, history, and identity of a people, then it opens the possibility for sharing

experiences, understanding the interests and identities of others, and communicating better in general. People are challenged to rethink assumptions about themselves and their lives as they encounter new horizons.[16]

Of course, music can contribute to the disruption and disintegration of communities and to a hardening of prejudice against real or perceived differences. Whether the links between music and community result in democratic outcomes depends on specific social circumstances. In chapter 2, I address two of the most important of these social circumstances: political action and power. The work that music accomplishes within and between communities depends on strategic use of political action and on power—on the variable capacity of different individuals and groups to control musical production, meaning, and use. One implication of the constitutive presence of politics and power in music is that the positive, democratic role of music may be derailed at the outset. Optimism about a democratic role must be tempered with a realistic appraisal of music as a competitive, contested, and conflictual arena characterized by power and politics, which can result in both democratic and undemocratic outcomes.

Chapter 2	Popular Music, Political Action, and Power

ACTING IN CONCERT can take three main forms, each representing a distinctly different kind of community-based political action through music. I call these forms confrontational, deliberative, and pragmatic.[1] A *confrontational* form of acting in concert occurs when members of one community use musical practices to resist or oppose another community. Music helps assert the claims of the community, which are believed to stand in direct opposition to the claims of others. Music marshals the energies of a community in a confrontation with another community whose interests are viewed at least partly as contradictory. Community members use this confrontational form of acting in concert to enlist sympathy and support for the claims of their community, to draw attention to their concerns, and to assure that the interests of their community take precedence over the interests of other communities. This form of acting in concert has a potentially positive role to play in a democratic politics as a way of enlisting support for the political agenda of a particular community, for publicizing a political issue, for drawing citizens into active participation in the public life of a community, and for galvanizing action on specific issues.

Protest music is an example of music used as a confrontational form of acting in concert. Here, musicians decry the injustices and oppression endured by certain individuals and groups and extol the virtues of favored alternatives. Although the music makes little or no mention of community as an organizing theoretical and practical concept, there is an implicit effort to create enduring ties among individuals who share commitment to a particular issue or cause. Typically, the intent of protest musicians is to oppose the exploitation and oppression exercised by dominant elites and members of dominant groups. Musicians typically couch their music in confrontational terms that draw sharp distinctions between the perceived forces of right and wrong. They attempt to advance the cause of members of a favored group, who are typically portrayed in direct opposition to members of one or more other groups, by promoting sympathy and support.[2]

Other examples of confrontational forms of acting in concert appear in the work of researchers who rely, explicitly or implicitly, on a Gramscian-Marxist framework for the interpretation of cultural politics. In this framework, relations between dominant and subdominant groups are typically treated as fundamentally irreconcilable. Popular music represents the legitimate expression of members of the subdominant group, who resist and oppose oppression by members of the dominant group. It is viewed as a mouthpiece of the people: a communicative arena where group identity and allegiances are defined and cemented, a site where resistance and opposition occur. While researchers within this tradition make little explicit use of the concept of community, opting for the concept of class, political action is typically cast in the confrontational practices of struggle, resistance, and opposition.[3]

Although a confrontational form of acting in concert can make a significant contribution to democratic politics, it is only one possibility among others. Recently there has been a tendency among some researchers to interpret political action through music in only this way. It is important, however, not to limit the strategic political options of popular musicians and others. Sometimes a strictly oppositional and resistant stance can produce beneficial outcomes. It may be satisfying existentially and appear to be the only reasonable option for political action in, for example, a context of extreme repression. But an oppositional stance may be counterproductive when it alienates potential allies and further fractures communities. Similarly, an oppositional stance may be doomed to failure when, for example, the choice is posed in either-or terms that mean winning outright over more powerful rivals.

Political actors, especially those in subdominant positions, benefit from the availability of strategies of compromise, adaptation, accommodation, and negotiation for creating new democratic relationships between dominant and subdominant groups.

In addition, framing politics as a struggle between two opposing forces may motivate the forced erasure of intragroup differences and struggles. Because group solidarity and cohesiveness are considered to be strategically important in a struggle with another group, internal differences of political belief and commitment may be viewed not as legitimate expressions of diversity but as a failure on the part of certain members to realize or acknowledge their true interests. In such a situation, dissident members may be silenced by a majority or a powerful minority. From the point of view of a researcher working within this confrontational framework, it may be tempting to interpret the role of these dissidents in overly simple terms of co-optation—the dissidents have been co-opted by the dominant group—or to drop them from the picture entirely.

Finally, framing politics as a struggle between two opposing groups may overlook the fluidity between groups. It sets up political relations in black and white terms that deny the presence of border zones.[4] These zones "between stable places" are not simply transitional spaces occupied by individuals who are in the process of shifting their allegiances (Rosaldo 1988, 85). They are social spaces of overlapping identity and interest where people choose freely to live and are legitimate in their own right. These spaces may drop out of sight in an analysis couched exclusively in oppositional and resistant terms because they cannot easily be cast in simple terms of right against wrong. Worse, they may be uncritically portrayed as spaces occupied by people who are being co-opted or assimilated by the dominant group. Although this analysis may sometimes be true, at other times it is a distorted interpretation.

The presence of intragroup differences and disagreements, and of border zones between different groups, suggests that we need to consider a framework of negotiation rather than an either-or struggle between opposing forces. This framework would emphasize intracommunal disagreements and differences and take better account of the fluidity between communities. Popular music would be viewed as a site and a medium for disagreement and debate over both intra- and intercommunal

identity and commitments. Music becomes, in this interpretation, a forum for political deliberation.

The *deliberative* form of acting in concert occurs when members of
a community use musical practices to debate their identity and commitments or when members of different communities negotiate mutual
relations. Although, by definition, members of a community stand on
at least some common ground, they likely also retain multiple differences of identity, interest, and commitment, which may emerge as disagreements and conflicts. Unless these are simply squelched, in which
case the community is undemocratic, members of the community must
engage in the communicative interactions needed to adjust for differences, negotiate potential compromises, accommodate each other, and
find or create common ground for action on shared interests. This is a
political process and a form of political action in its own right as well
as a necessary preliminary step to forging agreement on common interests and goals for action in other political arenas. In other words, politics does not occur only after the formation of community. The
discovery, creation, and re-creation of community may themselves be
a political process and a form of political action marked by debate and
deliberation over communal identity and commitments. This form of
acting in concert is also applicable to relations among two or more different communities. Music can serve as a communicative arena in which
members of different communities debate and negotiate the terms of
their mutual relations.

The presence of disagreement and conflict in intra- and intercommunal relations should not provoke surprise or consternation. The important question is whether or not members of communities are able
to engage in the debate and discussion needed to negotiate their differences. For some people, music provides an arena in which this debate can occur. Because music is both a reflection and a determinant
of the identity and commitments of a community, debate about communal identity and commitments may appear here as well as in other
communicative arenas.

It may be tempting to push this argument further and conclude that
all music experienced within or between communities represents an
ongoing deliberative form of acting in concert, but this conclusion is
mistaken. Unreflective, habitual reinforcement of communal identity

and commitment, whether or not through music, is not necessarily political. To deny this is to deny any meaningful distinction between social and political, private and public realms. While all social life is potentially political, it is not inherently so. Social life becomes political through disagreement, debate, and conflict when unreflective, habitual reinforcement of communal identity and commitments is challenged.

The character and shape of a community formed wholly or partially around musical practices depends on the outcome of the debates emerging from multiple differences and disagreements. For example, different rap musicians express different, sometimes contradictory, messages and visions in their music. They express various beliefs, attitudes, and commitments that reflect existing African-American communities and offer competing visions of what those communities ought to be like. Both implicitly and explicitly, rap musicians debate these competing visions through their music as they respond to each other and to their audiences. Because music both reflects and determines identity, this debate has an impact on the beliefs, attitudes, and commitments of members of different African-American communities and helps form the character and shape of the communities.

Tricia Rose integrates this insight about music as a forum for argument and disagreement into her discussion of female rap musicians. She interprets black women rappers as engaged in an "ongoing dialogue" with each other, with members of their audience, with black male rappers, with black men and women in general, and with dominant American cultural forms (1994, 146–48). The dialogue concerns heterosexual courtship, the importance of the female voice, and "mastery in women's rap and black female public displays of physical and sexual freedom" (147). Women rappers "challenge sexism expressed by male rappers, yet sustain dialogue with them" (182). Rose's dialogism is an important contribution to an understanding of music as a communicative forum in which varied ideas and behaviors are negotiated.

What I mean by deliberation resembles her dialogism in important respects. I opt, however, for the term *deliberation* for two reasons. First, Rose often uses the term *dialogue* to mean simply a conversation or "multidirectional communication" (1994, 148) rather than debate or negotiation, both of which are central to deliberation.[5] Apart from the meaning she gives it, the term *dialogue* implies a relatively harmonious, conversational form of communication. In contrast, *deliberation* captures the idea of political disagreement, debate, and discussion.

Second, I opt for the term *deliberation* to ensure its disattachment from the larger encompassing framework of resistance to which it is anchored in Rose. Although she appears to view dialogue as a distinct form of communication in rap music, Rose places it within a larger framework of resistance and opposition. She emphasizes repeatedly that black women rappers are "resistant voices in rap music and in popular music in general. . . . Like their male counterparts, they are predominantly resistant voices" (1994, 146). The language and sensibility of resistance dominates Rose's book. I want to ensure that deliberation stands alone as a distinctive, legitimate form of political action in its own right.

Both confrontational and deliberative forms of acting in concert begin from a presumption of divergent interests. By contrast, the possibility of pragmatic political action begins from the premise of shared political interests. The *pragmatic* form of acting in concert occurs when members of one or more communities use music to promote awareness of shared interests and to organize collaborative efforts to address them. A pragmatic form of acting in concert may involve the efforts of members of a single community to identify and address shared concerns collaboratively, or it may tie together the concerns of different communities in order to build a collaborative effort spanning them all. This form of political action is characterized by cooperative and collaborative efforts to engage in mutually beneficial problem solving. It involves power sharing and the building of collaborative working relationships with other individuals and groups within a community or across different communities. This does not necessarily require mutual admiration or emotional bonding, but it does require mutual respect—acknowledging the validity of others' claims and being willing to work constructively with others. Pragmatic problem solving means that people share a common stake in solving a problem, that they identify that common stake, and that they discover or create the common bases for acting upon it.[6]

One example of a pragmatic form of acting in concert occurs annually in Minneapolis. Each year, members of the Powderhorn Park neighborhood, led by the Heart of the Beast Puppet Theatre, organize a May Day celebration to celebrate and unify the diverse ethnic and racial members of the community, build awareness of shared concerns and problems, and develop the social ties necessary for addressing them. Live music is a central part of the daylong event. Bands representing different members of the community and various musical sensibilities play throughout the day.

The environmental statements of Sting, the popular pop musician, are other examples of a pragmatic form of acting in concert. Sting uses his music to draw attention to global environmental problems and goad action among multiple communities and nations.

Although the musician's role as community organizer for collaborative problem solving is an important one, the fact of diversity suggests an important caveat. Given the multiplicity of interests and commitments within the community, there are likely to be significant obstacles to collaboration. While recognizing that humans with diverse identities and interests can discover or create common ground, we should also acknowledge the potential for failure. In a truly diverse population, some differences may prove too stubborn for collaborative resolution, even when they are not rooted in mutually incompatible interests. Collaborative problem solving can be an important strategy for collective action, but it is only one strategy among others.

These three forms of acting in concert should not be viewed as mutually exclusive. In practice, it is possible and probable that they will overlap. In other words, the same musical practice might reveal characteristics of more than one form. For example, a concert designed to organize collaborative efforts on behalf of a community might include musicians whose message is couched in oppositional, confrontational terms. In addition, the forms may complement each other. For example, deliberation about communal identity and commitments to define common goals or strategies may be a necessary prelude to both pragmatic and confrontational forms.

These forms of acting in concert occur in many different social settings and situations, including social spaces traditionally viewed as political, such as town halls and party headquarters on election night; but they may also include less traditional forms of political arenas such as dance and concert halls, the social spaces created by the circulation of musical recordings, and outdoor spaces where musicians play for tips. In short, acting in concert can occur wherever music is produced and consumed.

Social criticism may be an element in all three forms of acting in concert. It can play a deliberative role by keeping dominant members of the community honest, destabilizing and demystifying assumptions about the community and its members, and provoking reexamination of communal identity and commitments. Social criticism can ignite explicit disagreement and conflict in a community that once had an undemocratic veneer of agreement and consensus concealing basic differences. It may also be a part of a pragmatic form of acting in concert. Social criticism may shatter outdated presumptions about historical animosities and incompatibilities among individuals, groups, and communities that block collaborative forms of political action. Social critics might point out the invalidity of these old presumptions or probe beyond received wisdom to uncover common ground for collaboration. Finally, social criticism is often a form of confrontational politics, existing alongside and fueling resistance, opposition, struggle, and protest. It may complement or be an integral part of a confrontational form of acting in concert.

Popular Music and Power

Although music can enable several forms of acting in concert, it may nevertheless have little value in making actual changes in people's lives. The outcomes of acting in concert depend at least partly on power. Rather than address power comprehensively and thoroughly, I will concentrate on those aspects of power that increase or decrease the potential in popular music for democratic political action. Understanding this potential would be incomplete without addressing some of the ways in which political actors are both constrained and enabled to imagine, pursue, and achieve democratic options.

Power, like community, is a much debated term. A common, although by no means simple or uncontested, distinction is between "power over" and "power to," referring to a sense of power as domination and constraint, on the one hand, and power as a positive capacity, on the other hand.[7] Power as domination refers to inegalitarian social relations based on differences of class, gender, race, and ethnicity in which certain individuals or groups control, in varying degrees and ways, other individuals or groups. These inegalitarian relations sometimes harden into undemocratic barriers to political participation and create a communal and public life skewed in the interests of the wealthy and powerful.

Power as capacity refers to the skills and resources that enable critical choice and successful action by individuals or groups. Here, power represents the means of overcoming barriers to political participation and democratic change. Citizens in a democratic community must share a capacity for appropriate and responsible participation in public life. Capacity in this sense means appropriate attitudes, abilities, and skills for participation in political life—including, for example, listening and speaking skills, tolerance for differences, and critical-thinking skills. In addition, citizens require access to appropriate communicative arenas for participation in politics, including alternative arenas as well as mainstream and institutionalized ones. In short, power as capacity refers to an ability to critically formulate and attain goals.

To what degree does popular music enable individuals and communities to formulate democratic ends and bring them to fruition? How is popular music linked to "power to"—power as an enduring capacity? A full examination of this issue also requires consideration of "power over" because individuals and groups hold and exercise a certain level of capacity by virtue of their enduring relations with others, which both enable and constrain choice and action. Thus, fully understanding a capacity for political action requires that we address both the constraining and enabling conditions.

Others have argued that popular music increases power as a psychological or affective state by energizing the listener and increasing a sense of efficacy.[8] A related argument is that music contributes to a felt sense of unity or solidarity that increases group members' courage and sense of efficacy. This outcome is often attributed to music tied to the civil rights movement and some kinds of union and protest music because the music nurtures courage and resolve in the face of adversity.[9] Although it is important to recognize this form of power, it is also necessary to acknowledge that it is a limited conception. It does not consider power beyond perception and feeling or as a way of manipulating an environment to produce desired outcomes and control the circumstances of life. Listeners who experience power as perception and affect can nevertheless leave a musical performance and return to an everyday life of relative powerlessness. Another limitation of this link between music and power is that the perception of increased energy and efficacy may be inarticulate and unreflective, thus increasing the likelihood that it will dissipate quickly rather than make a lasting impact on a person's capacity.

Popular music can be tied to the so-called three faces of power.[10] The first face, generally viewed as the most obvious and the most directly tied to power as domination, involves an attempt by one or more individuals to control the behavior of others. According to political scientist Robert Dahl (1957, 202–3), this form of power involves a situation in which "A has power over B to the extent that he can get B to do something that B would not otherwise do." This form is present in music when, for example, music producers attempt directly to control the work of musicians or a repressive government exercises direct repression and censorship of music.[11] But this is always necessarily incomplete control. Music, once made public, is selectively appropriated by different individuals and groups for ends that may or may not resemble the initial intentions of the musician. Moreover, musical meaning can be oblique and hidden, making successful control of its messages partial at best.

In some cases, overt or explicit exercise of the first face of power may be absent; yet it is clear that certain individuals, groups, or issues are effectively controlled in some fashion. When this occurs, the second face of power may be present. One example of the second face is an implied threat. For example, repressive governments in Eastern Europe and the Soviet Union before the late 1980s were usually able to censor rock music successfully using indirect, implied threats rather than direct intervention in the lives of musicians (Ramet 1994). In such cases, control, or domination, is exercised in implied, relatively subtle form compared to the first face of power. Yet the result is identical: some individuals are subject to the control of others, even if the forms of control are not directly visible.

The third face of power concerns people's perceptions of their own needs and interests. These perceptions may be distorted in a variety of ways by misinformation, propaganda, ideological control, or a history of oppression. Music, like other cultural forms, has an impact on the identity of listeners and can distort people's perceptions of their interests. Yet musicians can also break through denial and misunderstanding to a better perception of self, interests, and options.[12]

Music can be interpreted as a reflection or outcome of power relations. In the previous chapter, I emphasized the degree to which music both reflects and re-creates human identity and relationships, including those of power. Theodor Adorno's readings of serious and popular music are good examples. He interprets music in terms of what it reveals about power relations in a capitalist political economy. His polemical conclusions about popular music—that it is unoriginal and uninventive, banal and vulgar, constituting the "dregs of musical history," offering its listeners a "training course in passivity," and "undermining . . . autonomy and independence of judgment" (1962, 24–30)—all reflect his reductionist reading of the relationship between capitalism and popular culture, which he conceptualizes as unidirectional, with popular music capable only of reflecting, not determining, the course of history. Nevertheless, he captures an important insight about music as a kind of communication that models and reveals social relations of power.[13]

Finally, power can be connected to popular music as a communicative forum through which some people engage in political action. Music is a tool or resource that increases political capacity, especially for people who have historically been blocked from participation in more traditional and institutionalized political arenas. It thus increases political capacity by increasing opportunities for participation in communal and public life.[14]

Each of these ways of linking popular music to power is important and useful. For the purposes of exploring the theme of acting in concert, I will primarily use a conception of power as capacity that recognizes the importance of psychological and affective perceptions of efficacy and self-worth but goes well beyond perception; one that involves an ability to think and act in appropriate critical and strategic ways; one that crucially incorporates an ability to act in certain ways to achieve desired outcomes or, in other words, to make real changes in a social and physical environment; and one that recognizes the genesis of this kind of power in social relations, especially in culture and particularly in popular music. In short, acting in concert entails a conception of power as a capacity for critically formulating (democratic) goals and carrying them into action using available and appropriate means that produce the desired results.

This formulation has three key virtues. First, it entails the possibility of action—specifically, effective action, or action that produces a desired outcome—which goes well beyond conceptions of power that emphasize perception and feeling. Second, it requires the possession of means and resources necessary for successful action, thus recognizing that power is not a disembodied abstraction but tied to specific social structures, institutions, and practices that both enable and constrain human volition and action. Third, it involves an ability to act not on blind or distorted goals but on those that have been developed through critical reflection. This addresses the problem of the third face of power, which works against autonomous awareness and choice.

What are the grounds for this democratic capacity? How does one acquire it and use it? Within the discipline of political science, factors such as votes, money, and access to politicians are traditionally emphasized as the bases for political power. While these are important, they do not begin to exhaust the possible sources of power. Power is socially situated—dependent on specific social relations in particular historical and cultural circumstances. It is not inherent, nor can it be assumed. It is a product and factor of specific times and places and part of the mixture of enabling and constraining circumstances. This is consistent with a social psychology that emphasizes the ties of human identity to specific social and cultural environments, and power as capacity depends on the presence within a social context of means and resources that enable democratic action. Thus, the contribution of music to political capacity varies by context and circumstance, depending on the relative mix of enabling and constraining conditions.

Chapter 3	*El pueblo, unido* *jamás será vencido*

Popular Music and Democratic
Politics in Chile, 1960–1973

THE CHILEAN CASE is dominated by the confrontational form of acting in concert.[1] Understanding why this is so requires an understanding of key points in Chilean political history. Between 1830 and 1973, Chileans governed themselves democratically except for a brief interruption of military rule in 1924. The parliamentary system was relatively open and representative with a well-developed system of political parties, although it was controlled in large part by wealthy landowners and commercial and industrial businesspeople. By the 1930s, however, with the rise of a Marxist left within a highly unionized and politicized labor force, the party system became highly polarized, covering the full ideological spectrum and producing a vacuum at the center of political life.[2] Unable to gain effective majorities on their own, parties on the right and left entered coalitions with center parties, allowing the political system to muddle along despite sharp ideological differences. These coalitions tended to disintegrate soon after elections, when politicians attempted to position themselves for future elections by distinguishing themselves ideologically from their coalition partners. With little ideological or programmatic consensus, Chilean politics was characterized by debates about each policy decision, attempts to accommodate opposing sides, and protests by oppositional and dissatisfied groups. Although existing arrangements generally favored upper-class interests, each party benefited in concrete ways from the existing system. Therefore, through most of modern Chilean history, there was a strong consensus on democratic procedures, especially elections, if not on more fundamental issues of ideology and policy. The lack of a political center was exacerbated by various fractures in Chilean cultural life, such as the marginalized status of Quechua, Aymara, and Mapuche Indians; a gulf between urban and rural life; and the encroachments of foreign culture, which tended to ghettoize indigenous expression.[3]

This chapter explores the emergence and impact of confrontational forms of acting in concert in this fractured and polarized political context between (roughly) 1960–73. Important political changes occurred in Chile during that period, and the popular music of Chile both reflected and determined them. With little exception, music failed to help heal the great division between left and right in Chilean politics and instead contributed to widening it. In other words, musicians contributed little to the creation of a political community encompassing both left and right and perhaps contributed a great deal to undermining its possibility. This can be partly attributed precisely to the one-sided emphasis among Chilean musicians on confrontational forms of acting in concert, which increased the distance between left and right in Chile. Chilean musicians generally saw their task as organizing elements of the democratic left in order to oppose and resist the political right in what both sides largely conceived of as an either-or contest for power. These confrontational strategies were partly dictated by the demands of the political context of polarization.

Although it is not surprising that musicians relied heavily on confrontational strategies, it was nevertheless unfortunate. A deliberative form of acting in concert may have encouraged members of the democratic left to rethink and challenge their existing commitments, some of which fanned the tensions between left and right. Both the deliberative and pragmatic forms of acting in concert could have been used to promote a search for common ground. But if musicians failed to contribute to a healing of the divide, they did play a significant role in creating and sustaining subnational communities, especially on the political left, and increasing the capacity of Chileans for pursuing democratic options.

Two distinct forms of popular Chilean music have been christened "new song," a name that recognizes their ties to the social and political "new song movements" occurring throughout Latin America and later throughout the world during the 1960s, 1970s, and 1980s.[4] The first form to appear in Chile, during the early part of the 1960s, was dubbed nueva canción. Nueva canción musicians were active within Chile until the coup in 1973, when, driven into exile, they continued their work in other parts of the world. The second form, discussed in chapter 4, appeared gradually after the coup and in 1975 was named canto nuevo. A third form, also covered in chapter 4, served important political functions but is distinct from both nueva canción and canto nuevo. This form, canto poblacional, is tied to the *poblaciones*, or lower-class neighborhoods, of Santiago. Each of these streams of popular music played a role of social cement, tying some Chileans together in common awareness, commitment, and endeavor; and each provided a communicative forum for opening public spaces and acting politically.

Community Organizing for Resistance

During the 1960s, nueva canción musicians played key roles in the formation of a group of democratic socialists that emerged as a community of resistance and opposition. In other words, the formation of community and the use of confrontational forms of political action occurred simultaneously. The constituent elements of this community included a commitment to resistance and opposition to the political right, to cultural degeneration within Chile, and to other countries viewed as imperialists.

Nueva canción originated in the southern cone of Latin America in the late 1950s in a dual project of roots recovery and social criticism, and its musicians can be viewed as community organizers for the effort. The community itself was primarily made up of students, professionals, and marginalized populations. The project of roots recovery involved attempts to recover, revalue, and re-create indigenous cultural expressions. North American and European music was gradually suffocating indigenous musical forms such as tango in Argentina, son in Cuba, ranchera in Mexico, samba in Brazil, and cueca in Chile. Nueva canción musicians set out to rescue these forms by celebrating them and integrating them into their new creations. The "new" in *nueva canción* thus refers to a recovery of old traditions as well as the creation of new:

new was built on the old, forming a temporal continuity. Social criticism developed concurrently with the project of roots recovery. Nueva canción musicians attempted to organize a political community that could successfully resist injustice and exploitation within Chile and cultural and economic domination from the north. Songs were vehicles for social commentary and criticism—telling histories, denouncing opponents, extolling democratic alternatives, and relating specific incidents.

Recovery and social criticism took shape in the work of early researchers and diffusers of Chilean popular music such as Margot Loyola, Violeta Parra, Calatambo Albarracín, Cuncumen, Chagual, and later Rolando Alarcón and Victor Jara.[5] These musicians and researchers traveled and toured widely throughout Chile, finding indigenous songs, dances, and histories to perform and popularize and to form the basis for original compositions. Their task, as they saw it, was to "recover the past," to "recover the memory of their origins," and to find their "lost race."[6] In practice, this goal involved exploring and developing connections between not only past and present but also urban and rural, Indian and non-Indian, middle and lower classes, and Chileans and other Latin Americans. These ties would help bind together a community defined by mutual awareness and commitment to democratic change.

In part, nueva canción musicians created ties between past and present simply by performing traditional songs and dances, which marked the art forms as worthy of recognition. The musicians also integrated older indigenous forms and styles of music into contemporary creations. For example, Violeta Parra, Victor Jara, Quilapayún, and Inti-Illimani all experimented widely with the indigenous Chilean cueca dance rhythm. In addition, members of groups such as Quilapayún and Inti-Illimani began integrating native instrumentation into their music, especially the panpipes, charango, and quenas of the Andean Indians. Nueva canción musicians also included historical references in their original compositions. One prominent example was "La cantata Santa María de Iquique," written by Luis Advis and recorded by Quilapayún. The "cantata," performed for the first time at the Second Festival of Nueva Canción Chilena in 1970, told the story of a 1907 military massacre of striking salt miners and their families and exhorted Chileans to remember their history:

We will be the speakers, we will tell the truth,
truth that is the bitter death of the salt miners. . . .
We should never forget.
Now we ask you to pay attention.

The historical project of nueva canción chilena included recount-
ing recent events and critiquing them. For example, Victor Jara's
"Preguntas por Puerto Montt" [questions about Puerto Montt] (1968)
related the story of a 1968 military attack on ninety-one farm families
who had occupied a plot of uncultivated land near the city of Puerto
Montt in southern Chile, an attack that killed seven people and
wounded sixty. In the song, Jara denounced the event and the Chilean
minister of the interior, who ordered the attack:

You ought to tell us,
Mister Pérez Zujović,
why the defenseless people
were met with rifles.
Mister Pérez, your conscience
you have buried in a coffin
and you cannot wash your hands
with all the rains that fall in southern Chile.[7]

Nueva canción musicians also attempted to bridge the gulf between
urban and rural life by performing and popularizing music from the rural areas, making it available to urban audiences. They traveled widely
throughout Chile collecting material, which helped them establish ties
with many people, including the workers, miners, and students associated with growing radical political affiliations. One illustration was the
appearance of the folklore association Chile Ríe y Canta, formed in
1963 on Radio Mineria to help popularize nueva canción and folklore
in general. Financed prominently by worker and farmer syndicates and
unions based outside of Santiago, Chile Ríe y Canta eventually included
a radio program, a television program, pamphlet and brochure publishing, records, educational programs, festivals, a *peña* (a coffeehouse with
an entertainment focus), and the sponsorship of more than thirty tours
(Largo Farías 1977, 17).[8] Violeta Parra, in particular, recorded a large
repertoire of folk songs collected from rural areas of Chile. Stories of
her travels sometimes found their way into her original compositions.

In "La exiliada del sur" [the southern exile], she named some of the places that she had visited and described how she had left part of herself in each place:

> I left one eye in Los Lagos
> by casual neglect,
> the other remained in Parral. . . .
> My nerves I left in Graneros,
> my blood in San Sebastián.[9]

Many nueva canción musicians wrote or performed music drawing attention to the presence of Mapuche, Aymara, and Quechua Indians in Chile. In "Levántate, Huenchullán" [stand up, Huenchullán], Violeta Parra described the injustices faced by the Mapuche people and exhorted the people to stand up against them:

> Araucanians have a deep pain
> that cannot be silenced.
> It is centuries of injustices
> that they have all witnessed.
> . . . Stand up, Huenchullán.[10]

Although the musicians were drawn largely from the educated middle class, they attempted to develop ties with the Chilean lower classes. Many of their songs emphasized the injustices faced by members of the lower classes or celebrated the everyday lives of marginalized Chileans. Victor Jara frequently went into the poblaciones of Santiago to write songs about the lives of the residents. One of his most popular cassettes was recorded in 1972 after he spent time in the población Herminda de la Victoria. Several songs extolled the creative capacity of the marginalized workers despite their difficult circumstances. For example, in "En el Río Mapocho" [in the Mapocho River] (1972), he testified to the durability and good humor of the *pobladores* (residents of the poblaciones) throughout the rainy season, which drenches everything in the población. This cassette, like others of its kind, helped solidify within the poblaciones a sense of shared experiences while allowing a wider listening audience access to those experiences. In "Por qué los pobres no tienen" [because the poor do without], Violeta Parra sang of the plight of the marginalized classes and castigated those who would counsel peace at the expense of justice:

Since time immemorial
hell was invented
in order to frighten the poor
with its eternal punishment. . . .
And in order to continue the lie
they are called by their confessor
to be told that God does not want any revolution.[11]

Nueva canción musicians also attempted to form ties between Chileans and the people of other countries, especially those in Latin America. Nueva canción reawakened the concept of *boliviariana*, which connotes Latin American unity (Carrasco 1982, 23). Musicians consciously sought to create and perform music that was tied to the everyday lives of people throughout the region. For Latin Americans the songs were "a true mirror of their lives," in which "they have recorded all their hopes, their misfortunes, and their joys" (Carrasco 1982, 11). Nueva canción musicians recorded life experiences and shared them with others through festivals, concert tours, and the circulation of recordings and printed lyrics. Musicians in different Latin American countries borrowed freely from each other, integrating different elements into their musical expression. Violeta Parra's "Los pueblos americanos" [the American peoples], which she composed as an indigenous cueca, is a good example of this call for a Latin American unity. Addressing the peoples of Latin America, she sang:

The rulers,
they have you so separated.
When will it be . . .
that America will be
only one pillar?[12]

Many musicians admired the Cuban revolution and extolled its promises in their music. In "El aparecido" [the ghost] (1967), Victor Jara expressed his admiration for Che Guevara and his ability to circulate like a ghost among revolutionary movements in Latin America while escaping those who would kill him. Similarly, Jara's "A Cuba" [to Cuba] eulogizes the Cuban revolution and expresses solidarity with Cubans:

Hand in hand
like brothers

if you want me
I am here.
What more can I offer you
than to follow your example?
Commandante, compañero,
long live your revolution.[13]

Nueva canción musicians helped organize a community of demo-cratic socialists united initially by an interest in roots activism but quickly developing into a political community with an extensive pro-gram of resistance and opposition to the Chilean political right and to northern imperialism. The community straddled both urban and rural areas of Chile, and its membership included large segments of the Chil-ean middle, professional, and lower classes. Increasingly, the lower classes were incorporated into the political process, resulting, as we will see, in Salvador Allende's election to the Chilean presidency. Nueva canción musicians were partly responsible for this incorporation because they drew large audiences from the lower and middle classes to outdoor concerts and mass demonstrations as well as to recorded music. It is less clear, however, that nueva canción drew rural Indians into this politi-cal community, given the Indians' relative lack of access to musical performances and recordings. Although rural Indians' incorporation remained largely symbolic, many urbanized and unionized Indians grew more active politically, in part through contact with nueva canción.[14]

The ties drawn by nueva canción musicians did not extend across the divide between the political left and right. Given the explicit an-tagonism in many lyrics to upper- and upper-middle-class Chileans and their interests, it is not surprising that the hostility was mutual. It some-times took violent forms—for example, in physical attacks on Victor Jara and members of Quilapayún. An equally unfortunate form of hos-tility was the explicit antagonism of the mainstream press to nueva canción musicians. The conservative press frequently denounced Jara as a communist, losing "no opportunity to attack him and ridicule him" (Jara 1988, 126, 133). As a consequence, nueva canción musicians had little access to mainstream media, which limited the diffusion of their music, but instead reached their audiences through concerts and record-ings. Some of the most important social spaces for popular music were the peñas, which functioned as laboratories for emerging artists, diffusing folklore music and music reflecting the everyday lives of Chileans. The price of admission, however, barred people of limited means from attending. Musicians circumvented this problem by frequent tours, festivals, and concerts that were more accessible to lower- and lower-middle-class audiences.

Nueva canción musicians were motivated initially by a conscious commitment to explore their heritage, which included exploring indigenous contributions to a Chilean identity and affirming ties to these peoples. This involved appropriating musical instruments and forms characteristic of the Aymara and Quechua Indians that gradually became part of the nueva canción tradition. Today in Chile, the quena is the second-most popular instrument after the guitar (of Spanish origin); the bombo, panpipes, and charango are also widely used; and indigenous music and dance forms have been diffused among non-Indian populations. In other words, nueva canción musicians promoted the diffusion of some of the identifying characteristics of Andean and Mapuche Indians in the form of musical instruments, styles, and sensibilities. The cueca, quena, bombo, charango, and panpipes eventually became identifying traits of the community of democratic socialists that elected Salvador Allende. Playing and listening to these instruments and forms marked membership in the community.

I have thus far focused on the positive dimensions of this process: celebrating indigenous identities and developing a common core of identifying traits for the emerging community of democratic socialists. Some critics might charge that this process of roots discovery and recovery also raises troubling issues. First, the effort of some nueva canción musicians to discover their roots among marginalized lower-class, rural, and indigenous populations is somewhat disingenuous. With the exception of Víctor Jara, who emerged from humble rural beginnings, most musicians were from middle and professional classes, and most were descendants of white Western Europeans. Many, including the members of Quilapayún and Inti-Illimani, were relatively privileged university students. Most were firmly rooted in white, urban, middle-, and professional-class life. To say that they were searching for their roots among these other marginalized populations is misleading at best. This does not, of course, rule out the building of ties with marginalized populations.

Nor does it rule out the adoption by nueva canción musicians of these other identifying traits, however far removed they were from their own actual roots.

A second and related point is that the musical forms and instruments most frequently adopted by nueva canción musicians came from Quechua and Aymara Indians living in the Andes, who together represented a fraction of the total Chilean population. Instruments such as the quena and charango and dance forms such as the Peruvian huayno were drawn from native populations existing in very marginalized conditions in the Andean mountains in the north of Chile. Again, it is misleading to say that nueva canción musicians would discover their roots in such outposts. Instead, the process was as much about the *invention* of roots, and, by extension, a contemporary identity, as about the *discovery* of those roots.

In one sense, this is not a problem. People invent—as well as reinforce and re-create—their identity as they react to and absorb diverse influences. But this appropriation of the characteristics of marginal and indigenous populations raises a third issue. The quena and panpipes, once the exclusive cultural property of the Quechua and Aymara peoples and thus identifiable markers of them and their communities, are no longer their exclusive cultural property. Now that non-Indians engage in practices that once were exclusively Indian, what it means to be a Quechuan or Aymaran is more open to question, challenge, and change. The boundaries of Indian identities have become more porous and ill-defined and less subject to Indian control. Although this may have little immediate impact on the daily lives of most Chilean Indians, over the long run it makes cultural survival more difficult as identifying characteristics have become severed from traditional moorings. In other words, by organizing a community of democratic socialists, nueva canción musicians introduced a disorganizing influence into the communities of marginalized and indigenous Chileans,

Finally, by singing on behalf of marginalized and indigenous populations and exhorting them to stand up, the musicians can be charged with a form of paternalism. Although this charge is difficult to assess fairly, nueva canción musicians did make significant efforts to build respect for these populations while supporting a political agenda designed to promote their interests. Moreover, musicians such as Victor Jara,

Violeta Parra, Inti-Illimani, and Quilapayún, were especially popular among marginalized populations in Chile.

Although each of these criticisms has merit, all should be measured against the musicians' positive actions of promoting awareness of the lives of marginalized populations and advocating for improvements, attempting to create a community of democratic socialists and inviting marginalized groups to participate, and recovering and celebrating the contributions of these groups to Chile's cultural heritage. The musicians helped connect these Chileans to wider social and political movements, effectively developing a collective actor that achieved important, if short-lived, victories.

It may be tempting to find in the project of roots recovery a deliberative form of acting in concert, albeit a weak one. This, however, is a mistake. Although issues of communal identity and commitment were at stake, political deliberation—in the sense of disagreement, debate, and discussion about defining commitments—was largely absent. Rather, those defining commitments were largely taken for granted, and social criticism was turned outward to the Chilean political right and northern imperialists. At this point there was little evidence of a self-critical dimension that might have nurtured a willingness to mute the confrontational strategies of nueva canción and the community of democratic socialists. The confrontational form of acting in concert had already assumed robust dimensions in musicians' denunciations and attacks and would grow to even greater importance during the Allende presidency.

Allende and the Quest for Popular Unity

Party politics intensified during the 1960s. In 1964, the Christian Democrats, led by Eduardo Frei, won the presidential election. Claiming to represent a new and cohesive political center, and committed to a reformist strategy, the party attempted to break the political stalemate caused by the lack of a political center, breaking with its coalition partners and broadening its political base by organizing lower-class sectors. The strategy proved successful in some ways, especially in passing land reforms and instituting training programs for workers and peasants. It backfired, however, by alienating both right and center coalition parties and the conservative interests threatened by the reforms. The party also created anger and resentment on the left by making inroads into the left's traditional constituency. The left parties responded by intensifying their own efforts to organize popular support. As a result, party rivalry extended to even broader sections of the population.

In the 1969 elections, center parties, angered at the snub from the Christian Democrats, joined with Socialists and Communists in forming the Popular Unity coalition, with Salvador Allende as their candidate. Allende won with 36.2 percent of the vote, followed closely by the candidate on the right, Jorge Alessandri, with 34.9 percent, and Frei with 27.8 percent.[15] Even though Allende's mandate was well short of overwhelming, he quickly embarked on a course designed to initiate a peaceful and gradual transition to socialism. He nationalized key sectors of the economy, especially mining, industry, and banking; accelerated land expropriations initiated under Frei; raised wages for the lower classes; and increased social services in poor communities. Allende's policies produced strong economic growth during 1971. By the end of 1972, however, inflation had reached 164 percent, and the economy was hurt by U.S. cutbacks in credit and spare parts. Foreign-exchange reserves dwindled as the government attempted to fill the credit gap and make regular payments on the large external debt it had inherited from Frei. To compound problems, the price of copper, a primary source of export earnings, dropped to record lows.

A destabilization campaign began immediately after Allende's election. Financed in part by the U.S. government, the campaign included an extensive propaganda effort both inside Chile and abroad, massive demonstrations and work stoppages, and economic sabotage from commercial and industrial interests threatened by Allende's policies.[16] This sabotage was compounded by some of the actions of Allende supporters, such as unauthorized takeovers of businesses and factories, which contributed to the overall tension and distrust, and by internal conflicts within the Popular Unity over issues such as whether or not to attempt appeasement with the Christian Democrats, the appropriate speed of nationalization, and whether or not to use force against the advocates of a military coup.

Music figured prominently in Allende's campaigns and during his administration (1970–73). Given the mass media's hostility toward him, he was forced to rely on alternative means of communication. Both internally and internationally, music became a crucial information vehicle for countering the mainstream press's distortion of his record. In 1971, popular groups such as Inti-Illimani and Quilapayún began receiving financial support from the Allende government. They and some other musicians and groups, appointed to be cultural ambassadors as part of Operation Truth, were sent abroad to counter the anti-Allende propaganda in the media.[17]

Quilapayún, Inti-Illimani, Victor Jara, and others saw their task as unifying the left and building support for the policies of the Popular Unity (Carrasco 1988, 171). They attempted to fulfill this task through public concerts, developing closer ties to leftist movements and organizations such as the syndicalists, and organizing other musical and theatrical groups to perform for the Popular Unity. Recognizing the common interests of the Chilean and Cuban administrations and the importance of alternative means of communication, Castro sent a group of Cuban youth to study with Quilapayún during the Allende presidency. After Allende's election, Jara began setting up music and theater groups among trade unions in Santiago and in the countryside (Chavkin 1989, 224). Songs during this period saluted Allende's policies and characterized their likely results, transmitted electoral propaganda, and denounced opponents of Allende and the Popular Unity. In "Ni chicha ni limoná" [neither wine nor lemonade] (1971), Victor Jara ridiculed the Christian Democrats, who were afraid to compromise with the Popular Unity or to challenge the terrorism and sedition of the right.[18] The chorus was savagely satirical:

You are nothing,
neither wine nor lemonade.
You spend all your time
just massaging your dignity!

In another satirical song from the period, "Las casitas del barrio alto" [the little houses in the upper-class neighborhoods] (1971), Jara adapted Malvina Reynolds's song "Little Boxes" to Chilean circumstances, satirizing the life-styles of the rich. He added a verse referring to the Chile:

You smoke joints in your fancy cars,
play with bombs and politics,

and plot the murder of generals.
You are seditious gangsters.

These are hardly the sort of words designed to heal wounds and bridge political divides. On the contrary, their confrontational nature could be expected to further polarize right and left and contribute to the growing climate of distrust and agitation. One song from Jara's *La población* cassette, "La marcha de los pobladores" [the march of the shantytowners] (1972) testified to the optimistic and revolutionary spirit of the times:

Poblador, comrade poblador,
we will continue advancing until the end.
Poblador, comrade poblador,
for the children, for our homeland, and our home.
. . . now history will be ours
with a roof, clothing, and bread.
Let's march together toward the future.

Quilapayún song titles further illustrate the confrontational character of the music: "Tío Caimán" [Uncle Alligator] (1970), a spoof of "Uncle Sam," or the United States; "Venceremos" [we will conquer] (1971); "Marcha de la producción" [production march] (1971); "Las obreras" [the female workers] (1972); the cassette *No volveremos atrás* [we won't turn back] (1973); and "El pueblo, unido, jamás será vencido" [the people, united, will never be defeated] (1973).

Despite the efforts of nueva canción musicians and others, the Popular Unity ultimately failed to generate unity among the two-thirds or so of the population who wanted change in Chile. Christian Democrats and other moderates remained either uncommitted or opposed to Allende's strategies for change. More seriously, Allende and his supporters failed to create a substantial unity among the left, which continued to bicker about the pace of nationalization, the appropriate response to opponents, and whether or not to compromise with the Christian Democrats. Had supporters been able to achieve unity, the party could have acted more forcefully and cohesively in averting military intervention. In other words, the coup was not inevitable; the political failure of the left and the Popular Unity preceded the military in culpability.[19] Allende eventually proved willing but unable to bridge the gulf separating left and right. As the likelihood of a coup grew, he tried to move toward concession and accommodation; but his attempts to compromise were met with protests from coalition partners claiming that the transition to socialism was being undermined.

In short, although nueva canción helped form a community of democratic socialists in support of Allende and the Popular Unity, the community was deeply divided over strategy. Despite commonalities of interest in democratic change, awareness of membership in a community with a shared interest, and commitment to effecting change and a transformation to democratic socialism, disagreements about appropriate strategies contributed to the failure of its members to translate shared commitments and goals into successful collective action.

During 1972 and 1973, Chilean politics became even more confrontational. Mass civil disobedience, demonstrations, and counterdemonstrations were organized by both political sides, culminating in a huge strike and lockout in October 1972 by truckers, merchants, industrialists, and professionals. The 1973 elections, in which oppositional groups failed to win the two-thirds majority needed to impeach Allende, did not resolve the situation. Despite Allende's increased attempts to accommodate oppositional demands, a Chamber of Deputies resolution called on the military to protect the constitution and declared the Allende government illegitimate. The military took its cue and, two weeks later, on September 11, 1973, revolted and seized the presidential palace in an attack that killed Allende and some of his closest supporters.

The contributions of nueva canción musicians toward advancing the goals of the Popular Unity must be balanced against their failures. Looking back on the period, members of both Quilapayún and Inti-Illimani admit that the Allende years were defined by lost opportunity. Instead of using their music to build bridges between left and right, they opted to widen the gulf. Members of Quilapayún relate a revealing story in which they were invited to play at the popular annual Viña del Mar Music Festival in February 1973. This festival, held in the Chilean seaside resort city of Viña del Mar and attended primarily by its wealthy inhabitants, typically featured musicians who were either uncontroversial or aligned with moderate and conservative forces. But in 1973, for the first time, lower- and lower-middle-class forces from the

city's suburbs pressured organizers into inviting Quilapayún. Members
of the group initially saw the festival as an opportunity to "seek consensus rather than confrontation," to build bridges between the forces
on the left and right. As the festival neared, however, and the climate
of agitation increased, they changed their minds and chose instead to
play music with oppositional and divisive messages. Their singing caused
a near-riot (Carrasco 1988, 232–33). Members of Inti-Illimani offer a
similar self-indictment, saying that the group's songs during the Popular Unity period have been forgotten because they contributed "nada."
They did not broaden the social base of the Popular Unity and consequently did not contribute to the development of a political center in
Chile (Cifuentes 1989, 238).

Greater use of the deliberative form of acting in concert might have
enabled members of the political left to reexamine their commitments,
some of which blocked the possibility of compromise and accommodation with members of the oppositional right and contributed to the climate of hostility and tension. Similarly, the pragmatic form of acting
in concert might have enabled Chileans to discover or create common
ground among their extensive differences—for example, shared interests in economic prosperity, peaceful coexistence, and averting military
rule—and motivated collaborative efforts to achieve them. But as a result of a one-sided reliance on a confrontational form of acting in concert, nueva canción chilena contributed little to the development of a
community encompassing both the political left and right. On the contrary, musicians helped undermine the possibility of this community by
widening the gap. Did they have any choice? Given the many divisions
on the left and the nature of Chilean politics at the time, attempts at
compromise were likely to be met with howls of protest, as Allende
found out repeatedly. In addition, it is doubtful that any stance, con-
ciliatory or otherwise, would have convinced powerful and conservative elements that a gradual transition to socialism was a viable option.
Nevertheless, it is possible that self-criticism, conciliation, and compromise among nueva canción musicians might have helped avert the
military coup and the subsequent bloodshed.

Musicians did, however, help create some unity on the political left
and support for the policies of the Popular Unity, although they failed
to create a truly cohesive party or to lessen the divide between left and

right. The exact extent of their contribution is difficult to measure. Histories of the period emphasize the popularity among some segments of the people of musicians and groups such as Victor Jara, Patricio Manns, Quilapayún, and Inti-Illimani, whose public appearances were well attended and whose recordings sold well.[20] Their popularity lends support to the claim that musicians succeeded in achieving temporary "cultural preponderance" in terms of Chilean musical expression and consumption (Godoy 1981, 1). This marked an important shift from the growing dominance of imported forms of music and at least a temporary recommitment to indigenous creation. The musicians' prominence as cultural ambassadors and representatives of the Allende presidency also indicates their presence near the center of political developments. On balance, nueva canción provided a form of popular communication otherwise unavailable to democratic forces within Chile; and musicians helped cohere a collective actor and enabled its political action, even if it fell short of the democratic transformation envisioned by its members.

Chapter 4

Vamos a vivir

Resistance and Redemocratization
after the 1973 Coup

AFTER THE 1973 COUP, Chilean popular music played an important role in resisting the military's destruction of democracy.[1] The confrontational form of acting in concert remained central, in part because musicians had no choice: their strategies for political action were largely defined by the political context of extreme repression. Nevertheless, traces of both deliberative and pragmatic forms also emerged, especially in the poblaciones of Santiago.

One way to address the problem of a chasm at the center of political life is to eliminate one side or the other, which is precisely what the military set out to do after the coup. The junta tried to transform both the Chilean political system and the nature of everyday life by eliminating all vestiges of the political left. Combining brutal repression with bureaucratic management of government, the junta made a wholesale turn to the free market under the tutelage of the "Chicago Boys" (Chilean economists trained at the University of Chicago). Congress and local governments were disbanded, with elections at all levels indefinitely postponed. Major means of communication were either closed or subjected to strict censorship. Chileans designated as actually or potentially hostile to this effort, especially anyone associated with Allende's Popular Unity (including popular musicians and groups such as Victor Jara, Quilapayún, and Inti-Illimani), were exiled, imprisoned, or killed.[2] The junta ordered the destruction of books and records favorable to the Popular Unity and demolished DICAP (La Discoteca del Cantar Popular), the recording company of nueva canción chilena. The names of popular nueva canción musicians such as Violeta Parra, Victor Jara, and Quilapayún were erased from radio and television. Civic education, a regular part of the high school curriculum before the coup, was discontinued. After 1973 high school history instruction included no discussion of the Allende years or the struggles and movements of the 1960s, referring to Allende only as a Marxist head of state who led Chile into chaos. In addition to direct repression, the junta instituted many forms of indirect repression. For example, state support for the arts was discontinued, and culture was opened to the free market, increasing both the difficulty of earning a living as an artist and the privatization of cultural activity. Closing the media to dissident and alternative forms of music also made it difficult for many musicians to earn a living. Moreover, the effects of the political repression necessarily included self-censure.

Everyday life in Chile was dramatically privatized: public spaces were closed; political and cultural expressions were censored outright and made to conform to market standards. Loss of space for public and communal participation created social atomization and fragmentation, leaving Chileans cloistered in work and family and permitting little communication. The culture lost its expressive and communicative vitality, its plurality and innovative capacity, because repression strictly curtailed the acceptable range of cultural and political expression. The coup and the subsequent repression also produced a great rupture between past and present and between Chileans inside and outside the country. When the names of Salvador Allende, Victor Jara, and the Popular Unity were stricken from the history books and public mention, a temporal gulf began to develop, separating democratic Chile from the new Chile of dictatorship. Because a significant percentage of Chilean union leaders, activists, professionals, intellectuals, and artists fled the country (assuming they were not imprisoned or executed), a gulf also opened between Chileans within Chile and those forced to flee into exile.[3]

In sum, for a large portion of the Chilean population, especially the political left, the coup and subsequent military policies shredded social ties and connections. All social collectivities were threatened with disintegration. The repression and censorship undermined the communicative grounds for maintaining social ties and for sustaining a democratic identity. The community of democratic socialists formed partly by nueva canción musicians faced disintegration.

Surviving the Ruptures

For musicians and other political actors, choices were limited to the confrontational strategies of resistance and opposition to the violence of the dictatorship. The collaboration and compromise that distinguish a pragmatic form of acting in concert were impossible with a regime bent on eliminating dissenters and imposing its will across all differences. The debate and discussion that characterize a deliberative form of acting in concert were unnecessary among members of the surviving political left because the extremity of the situation left few alternatives other than survival, patience, and opposition. These are hardly debatable options. The result was a continuation of strict reliance on confrontational forms of acting in concert, although in more muted and subtle forms.

In the first several years after the coup, musicians and other artists attempted to maintain continuity in cultural expression and everyday life despite the violent ruptures introduced by the junta. Challenges included the overall lack of public space, the atomization of Chilean society and the related loss of close ties to social groups, the restrictions on language and expression in general, the absence of an economic infrastructure and the means of circulating musical products, and a lack of access to the media.[4] Musicians and groups such as Barroco Andino, Grupo Ortiga, Illapu, Aymara, Aquelarre, Wampara, Cantierra, Caprí, Isabel Aldunate, Osvaldo Leiva, Osvaldo Torres, and Nano Acevedo began opening new public spaces and creating new means of musical diffusion by participating in "concerts of solidarity" and playing in peñas and festivals. Although the explicit political content of their music was muted, the mere occurrence of these events indicated a refusal to accede totally to the junta's privatization of culture and closing of public spaces.[5] By the mid-1970s, the frequency of these events signaled the need to acknowledge a new form of "new song." In 1975 Ricardo García, radio disc jockey and organizer of the 1969 First Festival of Chilean New

Song, christened the movement *canto nuevo* (new song). Like nueva canción, this form blended the old and the new—old in its roots to tradition and history but new in its ties to current social reality.

Although the history of the 1960s and the Allende years had been officially excised from the school curriculum and public mention, it was nevertheless taught through music. Nueva canción tapes continued to circulate clandestinely. Some songs, such as Victor Jara's "Preguntas por Puerto Montt" and Quilapayún's "Cantata Santa Maria de Iquique," described real historical events. Others were so intimately tied to the historical developments of the 1960s and early 1970s that their meaning was necessarily connected to concrete historical events and processes of the period. For example, Violeta Parra's popular "Run Run se fue pa'l norte" [Run Run left for the north] was widely known to be her expression of remorse and grief after her lover, nicknamed Run Run, left her. Its performance was not likely to be viewed as directly threatening to the military junta because it did not treat explicitly political themes. Yet an initiated audience associated it with the personal life of Violeta Parra, who herself had become a symbol of a democratic Chile. Similarly, Victor Jara's cassette *La Población* recalled his celebration of the everyday lives of pobladores and his decrial of the injustices they faced.

Many canto nuevo musicians contributed to this historical project. By covering songs of nueva canción musicians, even if the songs contained no clear political content, they recalled the significance and meaning of those musicians and the political events of the 1960s and early 1970s. Most songs by Violeta Parra fulfilled this function. Because Parra killed herself in 1967, her name was not directly associated with Allende's Popular Unity. Therefore, singing her compositions was relatively safe, and many of them were widely interpreted after the coup.

Some canto nuevo musicians also engaged in social criticism of contemporary life in Chile. Throughout the 1970s, it was dangerous to do this explicitly. Instead, songs could be covered or composed with hidden, oblique, or metaphorical meanings available to an initiated audience. For example, an interpretation of Violeta Parra's "Gracias a la vida" [thanks to life] by a canto nuevo musician affirmed the beauty of life despite its many pitfalls and pains and metaphorically refused to accede to the horror and brutality of the military regime. Some of the songs covered or composed by canto nuevo musicians skated a fine line between direct and indirect criticism of social relations within Chile. For example, Aquelarre's popular 1975 version of Patricio Manns's "El cautivo del Til Til" [the captive of Til Til], which broke previous sales records for its recording company, told of a political prisoner named Manuel, a "guerilla of liberty." Although the song did not explicitly refer to contemporary events in Chile, it required some courage to sing; a listener needed little imagination to connect its meaning to the contemporary plight of Chileans who had been detained for political reasons. The group Ortiga performed the "Cantata de los derechos humanos" [cantata of human rights], written by the Chilean priest Esteban Gumicio and Alejandro Guarello. The cantata, presented on November 22, 1978, in the Catedral de Santiago under the protective umbrella of the Catholic Church, touched on central themes of human rights without alluding to specific rights violations within Chile.[6] Although musicians protected themselves by omitting direct references to events or circumstances in Chile and by working under the protection of the Catholic Church, they nevertheless placed themselves in some danger by singing and recording these songs. Detainments and disappearances were frequent during this period, and the execution of Victor Jara and the forced exile of other nueva canción musicians were vivid proof that the military junta viewed musicians as threats.

Canto nuevo musicians were able in relative safety to continue the project of drawing attention to the presence of the indigenous peoples of Chile, especially Aymara and Quechua Indians from the Andes and the Mapuche Indians in the south—for example, in Cantierra's 1978 version of Violeta Parra's "El guillatún," which describes a Mapuche harvest and religious ceremony, and Illapu's 1976 cover of her "Los Mapuches." Many musicians and groups also continued the nueva canción practice of adopting Andean Indian instruments such as the quena, charango, and panpipes and performing rhythms and melodies from that region—partly to continue the project of roots recovery, partly as a gesture of solidarity with indigenous peoples, and partly because by this time these instruments characterized an artistic sensibility shared by many Chileans.

By preserving memories of a democratic Chile, musicians helped preserve its history; and by preserving its history, they helped preserve remnants of a democratic identity. Canto nuevo musicians maintained a historical and cultural continuity between the Chile before and after 1973. Although their music could not address political themes tied explicitly to Chile, the mere mention of important names and events from the country's democratic past was an important, albeit limited, political act. Musicians also generated and maintained an awareness of others with common concerns and interests and a collective commitment to a democratic Chile. Thus, they helped to preserve remnants of a collective actor—the community of democratic socialists that had formed during the 1960s and the Allende presidency—despite its clandestine and scattered form.

Given the lack of direct media access, canto nuevo musicians were forced to create alternative means of circulation of music, especially through access to a burgeoning cassette market and in peñas. Peñas multiplied as musicians sought to open spaces for their work and as different groups within Chile attempted to create cultural spaces for public gathering. To some degree, the peñas represented attempts by already existing political and cultural communities within Chile to create venues for maintenance, expression, and circulation. In other words, after the coup the peñas were at least initially an effect, not a cause, of community. Their role, however, was crucial in helping maintain existing cultural and political communities within Chile, in part by maintaining memories of forbidden people and events and by providing a public space where community members could congregate.[7]

The circulation of records and cassettes provided a form of mass communication that was otherwise unavailable in the mainstream media. Cassettes, in particular, ensured easy and extensive dissemination of songs because they are small and easily hidden, cheap and easy to duplicate. Their availability and distribution increased dramatically, as did cassette players and recorders, during the 1970s and early 1980s. By 1987, 79.9 percent of Chilean households owned a cassette-radio, and 37.9 percent of households owned a cassette-recorder (Brunner and Catalán 1987, 61).[8]

In 1975, Ricardo García opened the recording company Alerce with the objective of "rescuing dispersed values" (Godoy 1981, 15) and with "the deeply felt sense of not permitting the erasure of what some call the memory of a people" (García 1987, 69).[9] Opening Alerce itself was a direct challenge to the junta and put García's life in jeopardy. Some canto nuevo musicians and groups turned to Alerce to record their music because they had no other recording options. Others, such as Ortiga and Chamal, rejected offers from other important recording companies in favor of Alerce to participate in this task of "rescue" (García 1987, 71).

Also in 1975, Miguel Davagnino, the former director of Radio Chilena, created the radio program "Nuestro canto" [our song] for Radio Chilena. "Nuestro canto" broadcast every night for four years (1976–80) and then became a weekly program, broadcasting indigenous popular music that included the work of canto nuevo musicians. Beginning in 1977 Davagnino produced a series of concerts to "create new settings for popular song" (Godoy 1981, 18). In addition to Alerce and "Nuestro canto," cultural organizations such as Agrupación Cultural Universitaria (ACU), Productora Canto Joven, Agrupación de Músico Jóvenes, and Taller 666 emerged to support musical production and expression directly or indirectly.

Although it is relatively easy to identify canto nuevo musicians, it is more difficult to identify their public. Data available in 1980 indicate that most fans were university students, professionals, and other well-educated individuals.[10] These data, however, are only generally indicative of the public because they were based on the attendees of a peña called Canto Nuestro. Thus, they reflect a class bias, given that most lower- and lower-middle-class fans would be excluded by the price of admission. The absence of economically marginalized Chileans from peñas does not necessarily indicate that they were unaware or unappreciative of canto nuevo. Moreover, the data do not take into account the fact that peña-goers returned to their respective neighborhoods with the new music, which they then disseminated to a wider audience not captured in the survey.

The Growth of Explicit Opposition

During the 1980s, the confrontational strategies of opposition and resistance, underground during the 1970s, surfaced in explicit forms. Goaded in part by deteriorating economic conditions in the early 1980s, and despite continued repression, Chileans more and more explicitly expressed their opposition to the junta. At first, this opposition took tentative forms such as banging pots and pans, blowing automobile horns, displaying posters of Allende and Victor Jara, and igniting barricades of burning tires in intersections. Given the toll exacted by a decade of severe repression, this initial opposition was splintered and disunified. More organized forms, however, originated in institutions such as the Catholic church (for example, in the program known as Vicariate of Solidarity, which attempted to monitor human rights violations and provide aid to families of victims of repression); the Chilean Human Rights Commission; and the Committees for the Homeless, which organized land seizures on the outskirts of Santiago in 1983.[11]

As collective insurgency grew and the military found repression more difficult, musicians began inserting explicitly political messages into their music. In songs, forbidden names surfaced, as in "Homenaje" [homage], Santiago del Nuevo Extremo's tribute to Victor Jara:

> We won't hesitate to offer you a song,
> a million voices
> will tell you that it was not in vain
> what you gave us from your mouth,
> the bread of air and a flower.
> Victor, great absent one,
> for all times we sing to you.

In "Yo te nombro, libertad" [I call you by name, liberty] (text by Paul Eluard), musician Isabel Aldunate referred directly to the problem of detained, tortured, and exiled Chileans. In "Vamos a vivir" [we are going to live], Nepalé set Allende's last words to music and advocated the freeing of detained Chileans.

Among the organized and coordinated forms of opposition that began to develop in the early and mid-1980s were *paros*, or national strikes, in which musicians often participated. For example, as part of the mobilization effort for a massive national strike in 1985, the cassette *El Paro Viene . . . Pinochet Se Va!!!* [the strike comes . . . Pinochet goes!!!] was recorded and circulated clandestinely. The musicians remained anonymous, allowing them to call directly for a national strike and denounce Pinochet. In one song from this cassette, "Avanzar, avanzar" [advance, advance], the musicians exhorted Chileans to

> advance, advance,
> toward the national strike,

to strike, to strike,
in order to throw out the general.

The lead was sung by a young man imitating the voice of Victor Jara, an apparent attempt to recall Jara and connect the struggles of the 1980s to those of the 1960s and early 1970s, in which Jara was directly involved. Another song from the cassette, "Ay sí, ay no" [oh yes, oh no], connected current struggles to the memory of "those who have disappeared":

Oh yes, oh no,
I agitate for the strike,
oh yes, oh no,
let's pass the word.
It is the people of Chile
that call for freedom,
. . . and those who have disappeared,
from silence they will return.

These forms of collective opposition involved widespread participation and contributed to a growing perception that a return to democracy was possible. Although music was not the only form of communication, it was available and accessible. Among opponents of the junta, canto nuevo provided a way to create and maintain awareness of a shared interest in, and commitment to, democratic change in Chile. In other words, it helped preserve and develop a collective sense of "we"—the people who opposed the junta and represented a democratic political identity. Playing and listening to nueva canción and canto nuevo represented identification with this democratic community while reinforcing and re-creating it.

Nevertheless, despite its partial revival during the early 1980s, canto nuevo lost much of its overall influence, at least among young people, to Chilean rock groups such as Los Prisioneros and to imported music.[12] The dilemma of canto nuevo lay in the tension between, on the one hand, its role of political remembrance and maintenance of democratic identity and community and, on the other, its tendency to become confined, in terms of mass appeal, to politically impotent nostalgia. Ironically, the role of canto nuevo in keeping memories alive also partly defined its failure. By looking backward it defined itself at least initially in nostalgic terms that failed to connect with the contemporary concerns of many youth. The dependence of canto nuevo musicians on peñas, recitals, and other concerts for performance excluded Chileans of limited means, thus contributing to a split between canto nuevo and the lower and lower-middle classes.[13] Unable to articulate direct political sentiments, musicians developed the poetic quality of their lyrics and the virtuosity of their instrumentation; ironically, these contributed to the perception that canto nuevo was too intellectual and elitist—an "art for specialists."[14]

Moreover, by appealing to students and professionals from the upper and upper-middle classes and by purging their music of explicit political themes, canto nuevo musicians began to add Pinochet supporters to their audience. From one point of view, this shift can be considered a failure because it weakened ties to the democratic left. But it also indicates that canto nuevo played a modest role in bridging left and right in the Chilean political landscape. By muting their oppositional and confrontational messages, whether or not by choice, musicians played to people with diverse political persuasions. They helped make it possible for Chileans on opposite political ends to come together in public spaces, beginning with concert halls and peñas. For example, in 1988, when nueva canción musician Isabel Parra returned to the country from exile, she played to a broad audience, not just to the old Popular Unity supporters. Canto nuevo musicians can be at least partly credited for this in that they had helped prepare the way. By bringing people of diverse political persuasions together in a public space, they helped make it imaginable that significant differences of political orientation could be set aside, at least temporarily, to allow for common meaningful experience. Whether intentionally or not, they created at least a slight opening for the toleration of political differences necessary to begin drawing ties across the great political fracture that so long divided Chileans on the left and the right. Although it would be going to far to say that canto nuevo musicians engaged in either deliberative or pragmatic forms of acting in concert, it can be said that they helped make these forms imaginable. They did not induce listeners to reexamine the commitments that identified them as members of a political community, nor did they seek common political ground across left and right. They helped make it possible, however, for members of the political left and right to share public spaces in amiable, nonhostile ways. They introduced a foothold of shared experience, a necessary prerequisite for developing greater understanding, tolerance of differences, and the identification of common ground.

Popular Participation in the Poblaciones

At the same time that canto nuevo was emerging in the peñas and on cassettes, another stream of popular Chilean music, unofficially known as canto poblacional, was flourishing in the poblaciones of Santiago.[15] Like nueva canción and canto nuevo musicians, many canto poblacional musicians shared the same political agenda and often engaged in confrontational forms of acting in concert. Especially within the borders of the poblaciones, however, many also turned to pragmatic forms of acting in concert to address shared concerns such as youth disillusionment, alcohol abuse, and money shortages for public projects. On occasion, some musicians also turned to deliberative forms of acting in concert, challenging members of both the political left and right to reexamine their commitments to mutual hostility.

Although not as prominent as nueva canción and canto nuevo, canto poblacional was more ubiquitous, involving more widespread participation and closer ties to the marginalized peoples of Chile. Musicians generally did not earn their primary living through music but were marginalized workers, artisans, and small-scale businesspersons. Their music expressed and commented on social reality, maintained a collective identity, and organized collective actions within the poblaciones to address urgent problems (Rivera 1980, 1983; Rivera and Torres 1981). Because it was rarely recorded and audience members usually came from the neighborhood, it generally did not circulate far outside the immediate locale.

Performances often occurred in conjunction with cultural and social events sponsored by organizations such as the Catholic church, local schools, and neighborhood civic groups. Sometimes, however, the music festivals and concerts were themselves the main draw. Rivera (1983, 5n; 1980, 43) estimates that some five hundred groups were active in 1979 in the poblaciones of Santiago and that, between 1975 and 1980, twenty to thirty "solidarity events," attended on average by fifty to one hundred people, were held weekly. While these numbers are impressive, they may nevertheless understate the full social and political significance of canto poblacional. In addition to playing a role in formal organized events, music is often an integral part of informal family and neighborhood gatherings in the poblaciones. Participation rates are high in these gatherings, which are oriented toward mutual enjoyment and creation of music rather than performance.

Like canto nuevo musicians in the peñas and concert halls, canto poblacional musicians helped open public spaces within the poblaciones where community-defining and -maintaining interactions could occur. They also helped maintain a sense of "we" at a time when the military sought to privatize and fracture Chilean society. Residents of the poblaciones used song as a way of sharing their sentiments about daily life and preserving and developing social ties. Although musicians frequently performed nueva canción and canto nuevo compositions, a large portion of their music was original, reflecting the everyday concerns of the musicians and their families, friends, and neighbors.[16] Often the music addressed the social conditions within the poblaciones, especially the relatively poor economic position of pobladores. In "Vi a mi rostro" [I saw my face], Carlos Castillo sang about the difficult times under Pinochet:

> Today I saw my face reflected in the window,
> . . . I saw the mourning women walking
> through the streets dressed in black.[17]
> And I also saw the thin face of hunger
> that is always present in the poblaciones
> and in the Alameda [main street through Santiago],
> inside the homes
> and on the sidewalks.

Similarly, in "Hace un mes" [it has been a month], Gloria Rojas expressed the despair of many residents of the poblaciones:

> It has been a month
> that I haven't eaten the daily bread.
> Today it has been a month
> since I lost interest in life.

Many canto poblacional musicians also composed songs addressing issues related to larger social and political arenas. Like the songs about specific concerns within the poblaciones, these songs reflected and reinforced common sentiments and beliefs among residents. Both Castillo and Rojas wrote songs paying tribute to Allende, whose memory remains for most pobladores a potent symbol of more hopeful times. In "Salvador," Rojas challenged the official histories written about Allende:

> The story that I was told about you
> wasn't truthful,
> thousands of mouths have darkened it.
> And I, at this very moment,
> would like to see you
> come and show yourself, Salvador.

Castillo's "Vi a mi rostro" included a barely veiled reference to Allende and his last words:

> Today I remembered
> the burning voice of the compañero
> who gave his life for us
> in the Moneda. . . .
> And I saw the grand Alemedas
> opening up for the very first time
> so that the new Chilean
> could walk through the liberated land.

Allende is "the compañero" with the "burning voice," and the rest of the stanza paraphrases his last words, delivered over the radio in which he said that "sooner rather than later the grand avenues will be open where free men will march on to build a better society."

In some cases, canto poblacional was used as a pragmatic form of acting in concert to promote awareness of a specific problem and organize members of one or more poblaciones to address it. During the 1980s, for example, music was increasingly used to counter the frustration and disillusionment of young people within the poblaciones, providing a positive form of social engagement, an expressive outlet, and a forum for educating youth about the perils of drug and alcohol abuse. Musicians such as Castillo and Rojas were frequently asked to perform during events that had practical goals, such as providing a positive social outlet for youth, raising money for school textbooks, or promoting discussion about strategies for improving neighborhood streets.

Although most canto poblacional musicians played entirely to audiences within their own neighborhoods, two groups, Sol y Lluvia and Transporte Urbano, attained widespread popularity among multiple poblaciones; and their work helped tie together some of the common concerns of pobladores. Sol y Lluvia, in particular, enjoyed a popularity that transcended the boundaries of the poblaciones, even drawing fans from higher socioeconomic classes. This gave them a unique opportunity to challenge ideological, as well as socioeconomic, boundaries. They took this opportunity and engaged in a deliberative form of acting in concert by questioning and challenging the defining commitments of different communities. For example, Sol y Lluvia's "En un largo tour" [on a long tour] (1983) challenged Pinochet supporters to go see for themselves the actual consequences for most Chileans of the junta's economic policies:

> At this hour, precisely, at this hour,
> you must awaken
> and drive the lies from your life.
> I would like to take you on a long tour
> through Pudahuel and through La Legua [two marginalized
>   neighborhoods in Santiago],
> and you will see life as it really is.

Although this song could fit comfortably in a confrontational framework, it also played a deliberative role by challenging Pinochet supporters to reexamine their beliefs about and commitments to free-market economic policies. The group's "Armas vuélvanse a casa" [take your weapons home] also played a deliberative role by challenging Chileans of all political persuasions to reexamine their commitments to violent mutual hostility. Members of Sol y Lluvia exhorted Chileans to

> take your weapons home,
> disarm yourselves,
> so that you can construct peace.

Similarly, the group's "Gorrión de amor" [sparrow of love] rejected violent solutions to Chile's political problems and affirmed instead a peaceful resolution:

Sing, sing, sing, oh sparrow of love,
I am going to go out with a smile
to the war and the guns,
I am going to throw some dirt
and a root of hope
into the hole of the cannon.

Although Transporte Urbano also composed songs that testified to the social and economic difficulties of pobladores, much of the group's music celebrated residents' attempts to resist despair and act politically in creative ways. "Lo Chacón" (1990) praised graffiti artists from the población Lo Chacón, who surreptitiously painted walls in Santiago with murals supporting pobladores:

The truth is being stamped on the walls
with a roller and some glue. . . .
The guys from Lo Chacón go leaping over the walls
of the neighborhood
spreading truth and reason.

While most canto poblacional musicians produced and performed their work in small-scale venues such as church halls, homes, and school auditoriums, both Sol y Lluvia and Transporte Urbano performed frequently in outdoor stadiums and parks that could accommodate large crowds.

Popular Participation in the Streets

In June 1989, a crowded city bus made its way along Avenida Urrurrutia, a major artery in Santiago. At each corner, passengers stepped on and off, jostling for position and seats. At one stop, two musicians carrying guitars stepped onto the bus and received permission from the driver to board without paying and to sing.[18] Wending their way to the back of the bus, they shouldered passengers far enough aside to create space and began to sing:

Workers of my homeland,
I have faith in Chile and its future.
Other men will overcome this dark and bitter moment
when treason seems to reign.

These are my last words,
certain that our sacrifice
will not be in vain.
Continue with the certainty that a moral sanction
will punish the felony, the cowardice and treason
of this grey and bitter moment.
You must never forget
that sooner rather than later
the grand Alamedas will be open
where free men will march on
to build a better Chile.

These were "las últimas palabras" [the last words] of Salvador Allende, which the Chilean group Nepalé had recorded in the early 1980s. Although not all Chileans remembered Allende with fondness, the bus passengers, most of them drawn from the lower and lower middle classes, could be expected to sympathize with his memory or even revere it.

The singers barely paused for breath before beginning their second number, Violeta Parra's "Y arriba quemando el sol" [and the sun is burning above]. Written in the mid-1960s, the song decries the oppressive living conditions of miners in the north of Chile. It blames these conditions on the mine owner, who "takes refuge in the shadow of the laws," and on the "slanted news" that hides them from people in other parts of the country. Although such an unhappy song may seem an odd choice for a crowded, jostling bus, it was likely to resonate with the passengers, most of whom were working-class Chileans facing difficult economic circumstances.

After they finished the song, the musicians passed a hat among the passengers as they shouldered their way to the front of the bus to get off at the next stop.

ON WEEKEND NIGHTS, artists, artisans, and street performers gather in the streets of Bella Vista, a neighborhood in central Santiago, to show and sell their work. Thousands of Chileans and a few tourists arrive each night to relax, shop, and enjoy the various forms of live entertainment. In July 1989, four young musicians playing worn and makeshift instruments, including a drum set made of plastic buckets and tin cans, set up their up equipment on a street corner. They began a song that connected their optimism for peaceful and democratic change in Chile to those people who had disappeared or were still imprisoned by the junta:

> My people are happy,
> happy and peaceful
> walking toward freedom. . . .
> *Desaparecido* [disappeared person]
> *Detenido* [detained or imprisoned person]
> *Desaparecido*
> . . . And you are here,
> and you are here to live,
> and you are here.

The references to Chileans who had disappeared or been detained reminded the crowd of Pinochet's victims and in a way made them present.

Next the musicians sang "Tanta gente que toma la micro" [so many people take the city bus] by Sol y Lluvia:

> So many people take the bus
> without knowing
> if tomorrow the sun will rise.

They followed with a performance of Sol y Lluvia's "En un largo tour." Because the street bazaar attracted a sizable percentage of upper-middle-class and wealthy patrons, it was a good place to perform this song, which challenges Pinochet supporters to visit some of Santiago's poblaciones to see for themselves the consequences of Pinochet's economic policies.

The musicians sang and alternately passed a hat among the crowd for payment. The size and composition of the crowd shifted constantly as people arrived and departed.

THE MUSICIANS in these vignettes opened political spaces in busy streets in downtown Santiago and acted politically within them.[19] In general the musicians and other participants were solidly committed to a confrontational form of acting in concert; their primary purpose was resistance to the dictatorship. Music was used to define a political community in opposition to the junta, not to find common ground or seek accommodation. Because, to a limited degree, it challenged Chileans to reexamine their political commitments, it also bore traces of a deliberative form of acting in concert.

In each scene, musicians invited others to participate in the political action, an invitation that many accepted. Members of the audience contributed by clapping and singing along, donating pesos, and simply listening. In the context of ongoing military repression (albeit considerably muted in 1989), each event represented a destabilizing presence and an affirmation of democratic politics. Each temporary gathering on a busy Santiago street both revealed a community of Pinochet opponents and supporters of redemocratization that was more durable and widespread than a temporary gathering of strangers and, at the same time, reinforced and partially re-created the community. The musicians and members of the crowd opened a political space long enough to reconstitute themselves publicly as a political community defined by its commitments to democratic change in Chile. The musicians helped define and re-create this community by enabling its members to become aware of each other *as* members of the same community, by reminding members of shared democratic values and commitments, and by enabling their public expression and affirmation.

Before the late 1980s, street musicians playing songs with political themes were rare because acting alone or in small groups made them vulnerable to military persecution. By 1985, however, more and more musicians with political intent began appearing in outdoor markets, city buses, subway stairwells, and busy downtown streets. By 1989, street musicians were common in many parts of Santiago.[20] Many of them sought to earn extra income; most were amateur, relatively marginalized economically, and drawn from the poblaciones surrounding Santiago. In other words, they were generally canto poblacional musicians.

The quality and style of the musicianship and the content of the song lyrics varied considerably. Some songs expressed emotions tied to everyday life, while others criticized social, political, and economic life. Still other songs, especially covers of nueva canción and canto nuevo songs, were forms of both remembrance and social criticism. Many of the songs heard in the streets were written by nueva canción musicians, especially Violeta Parra and Victor Jara.

Two other kinds of music were also fixtures on the streets of Santiago. Música folklórico includes a variety of types of indigenous

Chilean folk music such as cueca and sentimental songs about the beauty of Chile. Música cívica includes orchestral and band music performed usually in public squares. Neither form is political in content or intent, yet both played a role in redeeming public spaces in Santiago by drawing people into interactions in public arenas. Although this may seem trivial, it is nevertheless significant in the context of a political regime intent on destroying all vestiges of public life.

The street lends itself readily to democratic political action. Unlike a peña, it requires little or no money to enter (only bus fare from the población); and it is open to everyone. Anyone who wants to can stake out a street corner and play and sing, assuming a minimum level of tolerance by the military and the police. Whether or not the musician's political sentiments resonate with pedestrians depends not on power or wealth but on the content and quality of the presentation. Street music easily incorporates audience participation. Typically, audience members, numbering from a handful to a crowd, are encouraged to sing or clap along; and they often do so robustly, indicating both their enthusiastic support for the musicians' themes and their knowledge of the song lyrics. Physically, the space is more informal than a concert hall or a peña, breaking down some of the psychological barriers between performer and listener. If people are threatened by the military or the police, the political space can be moved elsewhere, to be reopened wherever the musicians play and people stop to listen.

THE DISTINCTIONS BETWEEN nueva canción, canto nuevo, and canto poblacional are not absolute. Many canto poblacional musicians performed the music and lyrics of nueva canción and canto nuevo, and many viewed their own work as contributions to the development of "new song" in general. Similarly, many canto nuevo musicians saw their work as a continuation of nueva canción, although under radically different circumstances. The distinctions between these streams of popular music reflect factors such as relative level of professionalism, whether or not the musicians were trying to earn their primary living through music, the social groups within Chile to which each was tied, and whether they were living within Chile or abroad in exile. While canto poblacional musicians were rooted in the everyday lives of the residents of the poblaciones, canto nuevo musicians were tied to a middle- and upper-middle-class audience, despite their avowals of solidarity with marginalized Chileans. Originating primarily within the educated middle classes, nueva canción musicians sang primarily on behalf of the lower and lower-middle classes. After the coup, they lost their direct connections to specific social classes within Chile but remained popular through the circulation of recordings within some segments of Chilean society while developing new ties abroad.[21]

Although canto poblacional musicians were marginal in terms of mass appeal, by virtue of their ubiquitous presence, sheer numbers, and close ties to everyday life in the poblaciones, they were in some ways more important and influential than either nueva canción or canto nuevo musicians. They were social organizers, expressers of common experiences and sentiments, social critics and cementers of social bonds—roles that enabled them to contribute to the development and maintenance of local communities within the poblaciones. Moreover, canto poblacional was in some respects more democratic than nueva canción and canto nuevo, inviting greater participation, avoiding class barriers to that participation, and breaking down barriers between musician and listener.

Democratic Change?

It is relatively easy to demonstrate the commitment of musicians to democratic change and community but much more difficult to assess their actual impact on the political capacity of marginalized Chileans. Much of the evidence is indirect or inferred. Positive contributions can be summarized in terms of the formation and maintenance of democratic community and the outcomes of political action undertaken by members of that community.

First, during the 1960s, nueva canción musicians revitalized indigenous cultural creation while engaging in social criticism to draw attention to injustices within Chilean society and worldwide. Recovering and revaluing indigenous expressions threatened by the flood of cultural imports helped affirm among some Chileans a sense of "who we are" and rescued indigenous expressions such as the cueca from extinction.

Second, nueva canción musicians identified and challenged inequities within Chilean society, efforts that culminated in the gradual creation of a community of democratic socialists committed to democratic transformation.

Third, nueva canción musicians played an important role in Salvador Allende's election and during his administration. When Allende was excluded from and condemned by the mass media, their music offered an alternative communicative arena. Although his turbulent presidency ended suddenly and violently, the success of nueva canción musicians in securing and using this temporary base of institutional power must be acknowledged.

Fourth, immediately after the coup, the primary political role of canto nuevo and canto poblacional musicians was to preserve memories of a democratic Chile and their cultural heritage. During performances, they maintained and regenerated a collective "we" that countered the junta's attempt to atomize Chilean society, thus keeping a collective democratic identity alive. The importance of this task can be better appreciated if it is weighed against the alternative of a disappearing democratic identity. Chileans, like others, can create and recreate their political realities based only on imaginable alternatives. Maintaining a democratic identity helped democracy survive as an imaginable alternative. It was an essential prerequisite for redemocratization in Chile.

Fifth, in the late 1970s and early 1980s, canto nuevo and canto poblacional musicians began to criticize current conditions within Chile, although carefully and in muted terms. In other words, political music played more than a strictly defensive role after the coup. Its criticism of the injustices facing marginalized Chileans and of military cruelty built an awareness of common values and commitment to democracy among different sectors of Chilean society and made it more difficult for the upper and upper middle classes to forget the lives of the marginalized among them.

Sixth, although data are unavailable to support this claim, it seems reasonable to assume that the many pragmatic uses of music within the poblaciones resulted in some positive outcomes. If this is correct, canto poblacional musicians can be credited with increasing the ability of residents to solve or alleviate some of their social problems, such as alcoholism, shortage of school textbooks, and alienation and frustration among youth.

Finally, there are visible signs of the enduring significance of popular song. Chileans did not forget Allende and his Popular Unity, nor did they forget Victor Jara and his artistry. On the contrary, images of Allende and Jara, especially, remain prominent in Chile's cultural and political landscape. The popularity of "new song" musicians and groups such as Inti-Illimani, Illapu, Quilapayún, Isabel and Angel Parra, and Patricio Manns is also striking. Their recorded music continues to sell well to various age groups, and their concerts, frequently held in large stadiums, often sell out. How much is politically impotent nostalgia and how much actually contributes to a democratic Chile are questions difficult to gauge. The musicians' prominence and the enthusiastic response of their audiences do suggest that popular musicians have helped keep alive the democratic ideal—a substantial contribution, however difficult to measure. At a minimum, we can say that Chilean popular musicians helped ensure the possibility of extending and deepening the democratic ideal in Chile.

These contributions to the political capacity of marginalized Chileans must be balanced against the failures. The songs of nueva canción musicians were little match for the tanks and rifles of the military, which succeeded in carrying out most of its agenda. Cultural expression was largely privatized, musicians and other artists were forced to scramble to survive in a market increasingly flooded with foreign cultural expressions, and Chilean society as a whole became increasingly privatized and depoliticized. The daily lives of Indians and pobladores changed little, perhaps worsening since the early 1960s. Although Pinochet was defeated in the 1988 plebescite, he lost by a narrow margin of 55 to 43 percent, demonstrating his continuing popularity and indicating that the chasm at the center of Chilean political life remained.[22]

The emphasis of Chilean popular musicians on a confrontational form of acting in concert may have played a part in limiting their contributions. Before 1973, the preponderance of this form made sense in the context of a society polarized between left and right, with tensions and hostilities at high points. It is not surprising that nueva canción musicians simply internalized the oppositional sentiments and strategies endemic to this polarized context. While their exclusive use of the confrontational form is understandable, it is nevertheless regrettable, as some have admitted.

In the immediate years after 1973, heavy reliance on a confrontational form of acting in concert was a matter of simple necessity defined in reaction to a brutal, hostile regime. It is hard to imagine how musicians could have found common ground for collaboration with a military regime intent on brutally imposing its will across all political differences. It is also difficult to imagine the point of deliberation among members of the political left whose main political options amounted basically to subtle opposition, silence, adherence to the junta's wishes, and exile or death. Deliberation implies real alternatives to be weighed, discussed, and debated. The pressing political agenda of survival and maintenance of a democratic identity was defined for canto nuevo musicians by their context of brutal repression. Later, during the early and mid-1980s, it is possible that confrontational forms of political action could have been complemented by invitations to reconsider longstanding animosities and hostilities. Popular musicians might have made a greater effort to do this via deliberative and pragmatic forms of political action but generally did not.

Chapter 5

Laissez les bon temps roulez

Cajun Music and Cultural Revival

Unlike the Chilean case, the Cajun case is noteworthy for the prominence of both pragmatic and deliberative forms and the near absence of the confrontational form of acting in concert. The word *Cajun* is an Anglicized rendition of *Cadien*, which is a shortened version of *Acadien*, the French word for "Acadian," and refers to the white francophone people and culture of southwest Louisiana. Cajun music should not be confused with the zydeco music of black Creoles—persons of mixed African and French heritage in southwest Louisiana. Although the two kinds of music have much in common, they are distinct.[1]

Cajuns use a pragmatic form of acting in concert to address shared problems, especially economic marginalization, ethnic stigma, and cultural assimilation. They use a deliberative form to debate the relative merits of cultural preservation versus change and to negotiate their relations with black Creoles in the region. This chapter addresses the pragmatic form, chapter 6 the deliberative.

Understanding the role that each form plays in Cajun life requires that the historical relation between music, identity, and community be established. Although many outsiders mistakenly view Cajuns as homogeneous, their differences are as pronounced as their similarities. Cajuns have used music as a tool for fashioning community *from* diversity. They have made a virtue of disparate cultural, ethnic, and racial influences, forging them into the distinctive expression known as Cajun

79

music, which both reflects and sustains their identity. A form of social cement, the music has held them together through attempts to disperse them and through twentieth-century assimilation pressures.

Cajun Music As Social Cement

As a music of everyday life, Cajun music both reflects and partly determines Cajun history. As "art in the hands of the people" (Ancelet 1984, 151), Cajun music both reveals the identity of its people and serves as a communicative forum through which Cajuns fashion their history, their culture, and ultimately themselves.[2] Cajun musicians helped create a common identity from disparate cultural, ethnic, and racial influences in southern Louisiana. Cajun music played a role in cementing these diverse elements in Cajun life together and in partially counteracting the social and political forces pulling them apart.

French and African influences predominate in Cajun music. Between 1632 and 1654, several hundred peasant farmers from the westcentral French provinces sailed for Acadia in what is now Nova Scotia, many of them fleeing ongoing fighting between Catholics and Protestants. By 1713, when the Treaty of Utrecht ceded France's Acadia to Great Britain, the French Acadians numbered approximately 2,500. The British, who initially guaranteed the Acadians neutrality in future French-British conflicts as well as freedom of religion and cultural practice, increasingly viewed them as a dangerous foreign population jeopardizing British security interests during French-British hostilities. In 1755, the Acadians, by then numbering more than 12,000, were ordered to swear allegiance to Great Britain or face deportation. Most refused to swear allegiance.[3]

Resistance proved unsuccessful. Between 1755 and 1765 most of the Acadians were deported in several stages to England; to British Atlantic seaboard colonies such as Maryland and Pennsylvania, where they faced francophobia and anti-Catholicism induced in part by wars with France; and to France, where they were treated like peasants, an identity that they had shed long ago. Unhappy in their new circumstances and unwilling to accept the separation imposed by dispersal, many Acadians formulated plans to reunite. Several thousand eventually emigrated to Louisiana, established as a French colony in 1699 but ceded to Spain in 1762. Eager to settle the colony, the Spanish administrators welcomed them.

In Louisiana, the Acadians joined French, Spanish, German, Scotch, Irish, and Anglo settlers; the Chitimaches, Houmas, and Attakapas Indian tribes; slaves from the west coast of Africa brought to the colony between 1719 and 1809; *gens libres de couleur* (free people of color) emigrating from Haiti before and after the Haitian Revolution; Caribbean French slaves brought by exiled French planters from Cuba; and slaves brought from Virginia and Maryland. Class differences further complicated this ethnic and racial mix. Although the majority of Louisiana settlers were farmers of relatively modest means, a colonial elite consisting largely of white Creoles (planters and French military officers) held most of the political and economic power.

The Acadian settlers brought their music and dance with them to Louisiana. Various observers of Acadian life in Louisiana since 1765 have remarked on the importance of the weekly neighborhood dances in renewing and cementing social bonds.[4] During the nineteenth century, popular *bals de maison* (house dances), held every Saturday night, formed the centerpiece of Acadian social life. The large number of dance halls in the early twentieth century testified to the enduring social importance of Cajun music and dancing. These dances, along with *boucheries* (communal butcherings) and other social events, "reinforced sociocultural bonds between members of the Acadian community" (Brasseaux 1992, 28). They drew the Acadians into regular social interactions in which defining elements of their communities were re-created.

In addition to dance music, performed primarily on fiddle and percussion instruments such as spoons, the Acadians brought a wealth of ballads, often sung a capella by women. Many of these ballads originated in France, were taken to Nova Scotia, and subsequently went to Louisiana, where they remain in the Cajun repertoire, although sometimes under different names and with adapted lyrics and melodies. Agnes Bourque's "La veuve de sept ans" [the seven years' widow] originated in France and reflects a theme common in French folk music: the soldier's return. The seven years mentioned in the title was the length of time that French men had to serve in the army both before the French Revolution and during Napoleon's reign (Stanford and

Stanford 1974, 1). Bourque adapted the song to relate a true story about her grandfather during and after the American Civil War. Another elderly Cajun balladeer, Odile Falcon, sang ballads written more than four hundred years earlier in Normandy, Brittany, and Poitou (Fontenot 1983). The songs, which she learned from her grandparents, tell stories resonating with Cajun history of love, separation, and death.[5]

The aesthetics of Cajun music also reflect history, as is evident in the sound of the fiddle and accordion. In dances at home and in dance halls, the fiddle predominated throughout the nineteenth century. Playing without electronic amplification, fiddlers had to bear down hard on the strings to be heard over the din of the crowd. They also increased their volume by playing constant doublestops—two strings at once. The need to project the sound over the noise of a boisterous crowd also explains the development of the distinctive Cajun vocal style of singing energetically in high registers.

The accordion, invented in 1828 in Vienna, had made inroads into Cajun culture by the turn of the twentieth century and gained predominance by the 1920s. The type adopted by the Cajuns was a single-row diatonic accordion with four reed banks, giving it a loud, full, raucous sound. Compared to the larger and more elaborate chromatic accordion, this one is small and compact, light and relatively inexpensive. With a built-in bass section, its imperviousness to humidity, and its loud volume, it was attractive to Cajun musicians playing in the unamplified settings of humid Louisiana. Because a single-row diatonic accordion includes only the notes in a single scale, however, players were limited to relatively simple melodies in two or three keys. This made it necessary for musicians to compress their repertoire to fewer keys and simple melodies. The most common accordion key is C, a difficult one for fiddlers. Fiddlers quickly adapted by tuning their instrument down one whole step, making it possible to match the accordion while playing as if they were in the comfortable key of *D*. The retuned fiddle has a darker sound than a regularly tuned fiddle, which adds to the distinctive sound of Cajun music.

Another limitation of the single-row diatonic accordion is that it only has two chords on the left hand (unlike a full 120–bass piano accordion, which has the full range of major, minor, seventh, diminished, and augmented chords), even though many Cajun songs contain three or more chords. Moreover, like the melody buttons on the right side, the chord that is actually sounded by the instrument depends on whether the musician is pulling or pushing on the bellows. The accordionist may be playing a phrase that, harmonically speaking, requires a C chord; but if the bellows is going the wrong direction, that chord is not available. The result is a raucous dissonance as the accordion player competes almost randomly with the more harmonically consistent and appropriate chords of the other musicians.

Frequent doublestops and the dark sound of the retuned fiddle; the distinctive, high-register, male vocals; the raucous sound of the accordion; and other elements, such as the triangle fashioned from hay rake tines, became identifying characteristics of Cajun music. As listeners and participants came to recognize and identify with these sounds, they also became identifying characteristics of the people, both for Cajuns and for outsiders. This association has not always been favorable for either the music (which detractors called "chanky-chank") or the Cajun people. Ironically, however, those same detractions—particularly the music's raucousness—attract many non-Cajun listeners today.

Through their ballads and instrumental dance music, Cajun musicians maintained ties to France and to Nova Scotia by promoting common memories of a heritage rooted there. Singing of themes tied ultimately to France and Nova Scotia, in French, helped Cajuns maintain their partially French heritage. At the same time, new Cajun experiences in new circumstances were reflected in Cajun music, and Cajun music helped make these new experiences sensible and meaningful through creative expression. During the late nineteenth and early twentieth centuries, poor Cajuns (the vast majority) interacted closely with black Creoles, their fellow tenant farmers, despite concurrent pressure for segregation. From this interaction came the second primary influence in Cajun music, the African, which appeared in the form of blues sentiments and expressions, percussive and rhythmic techniques, syncopation, and vocal and instrumental improvisation.

Although Cajun music is noted for its lively, upbeat sound, it also has a distinct blues quality, which musicians acquired partly from Canray Fontenot, Alphonse "Bois-sec" Ardoin, Amédée Ardoin, and other black Creole musicians. Cajun musicians also learned to improvise, both vocally and instrumentally, from black Creole musicians such as Amédée

Ardoin, who improvised many of their lyrics and instrumental patterns in live performance. From Ardoin, Adam Fontenot, and others, Cajun musicians developed a syncopated accordion style, and they incorporated African-Caribbean rhythms and vocal lines derived from sources such as black Creole and African-American field hollers and West Indies work songs. Cajun musicians have often testified to this influence. Octa Clark says that he composed blues songs after hearing black Creoles singing in the fields. His longtime music partner, Hector Duhon, acknowledges a similar debt: "Tenant farmers would come up to the store. My old daddy would give them something to play. You'd also hear them singing in the fields, spirituals, hollers and yells. It was beautiful the way they sang" (Ancelet and Spitzer 1982).

The blues in Cajun music also emerged from the economic marginalization of many Cajuns. Although the original Acadian settlers were farmers of modest but comfortable means, the majority were downwardly mobile through the nineteenth century and into the twentieth. This downward mobility was politically influenced. For example, the colonial political and administrative system, staffed primarily by wealthy white Creole appointees, reinforced initial class differences. Most Acadians were disenfranchised by the original Louisiana state constitution adopted in 1812, which required property for voting, and by the fact that politics was conducted in English, which for most Acadians was a foreign language. Anglo Americans dominated postbellum and Reconstruction-era Louisiana, a period that saw declining economic fortunes for most Acadians, who suffered when southwest Louisiana entered an economic recession at the end of the Civil War that did not lift until World War II. Many were forced to sell their land due to default or taxes, and the Acadian planter class nearly disappeared. What remained was a small upper and upper-middle class of assimilating Acadians and the vast majority of impoverished Acadians who remained Acadian—the Cajuns. Anglo Americans used the term indiscriminately to include members of other ethnic and racial groups such as poor prairie black Creoles, poor Anglos, and nineteenth-century French immigrants. Eventually, Scots, Irish, Germans, Spanish, and Native Americans were also incorporated into the Cajun category, especially through intermarriage.[6]

Most Cajun musicians have not had the luxury of depending on music for their livelihood. Most have been tenant farmers, small-scale merchants, mechanics, day laborers, and jacks-of-all-trades. Dewey Balfa, perhaps the most famous Cajun musician of the past thirty years, farmed, drove a bread truck, sold insurance and furniture, and drove a school bus. One of the best-known and most beloved accordionists, Nathan Abshire, operated the Basile city dump. Abshire wrote many songs with titles such as "Pine Grove Blues," "Service Blues," "French Blues," "Off-shore Blues," and "Popcorn Blues." The repertoire in general is full of songs such as "Travailler c'est trop dur" [working is too hard], through which musicians have expressed their emotions about economic marginalization and its consequences.

Rarely have Cajun musicians transformed these blues expressions into direct political expression. Like the blues, the politics of Cajun music tend to be indirect and subtle, buried beneath layers of sugges-tion and metaphor. Themes such as hardship, broken families, lost love, and poverty sometimes reveal an underlying politics of economic marginalization. For example, "J'ai fait la tour de grand bois" [I went all around the big woods] tells of a young man prevented from court-ing because of his poverty. "How can I marry?" he wants to know. He is so poor that the parents of his beloved chase him away.[7] In addition to incorporating blues lyrics, the singer may inject wails and vocal breaks invoking sorrow and pain, and instrumentalists often play the flatted third and seventh notes of the blues scale.

The point of these bluesy Cajun songs is not to motivate change but to express emotion, to lament and moan, to console, and to solicit sympathy and camaraderie. They recall common experiences and sen-timents and express feelings to which many listeners can relate. By re-lating the experiences of a particular socioeconomic class, the songs promote an awareness of a shared class identity. Although they express the struggle of an economically marginalized people to survive in an often hostile environment, it is only rarely a struggle against explicitly identified individuals or groups, such as other social classes.

Other influences on the development of Cajun music were the in-digenous people of Louisiana, from whom musicians borrowed styles of singing and drumming; the Spanish, from whom they borrowed the gui-tar and a few melodies; the Anglos, from whom they borrowed lyrics translated into French as well as jigs and reels adapted for songs; the

Germans, from whom they borrowed the diatonic accordion. One striking example of this blend of influences was Dennis McGee's early twentieth-century version of the traditional "Valse du vacher" [cowboy's waltz]. A Cajun of Scotch, French, and American Indian descent, McGee uses a blues song derived from a French mazurka to describe the lonely life of a cowboy (Ancelet 1989, 19).

By the 1920s, the elements of Cajun music and the core repertoire defined as traditional were in place. Instrumentally, the diatonic accordion and fiddle dominated, accompanied by guitar and triangle or spoons. Singers worked at the top of their vocal ranges, emphasizing intensity of feeling rather than subtlety. Most lyrics considered love, lost love, unrequited love, hardship, and difficult times. In the 1920s and 1930s this sound and repertoire congealed when national recording companies such as Decca, Columbia, RCA, Victor, and Bluebird began recording regional and ethnic music to expand their markets for phonographs and records. Although musicians improvised vocally and instrumentally at live performances, the recordings standardized the lyrics and the style. The development of radio also contributed to the tradition by highlighting certain trends, sounds, and styles.[8]

Cajuns entered the twentieth century poor, isolated, and stubbornly francophone. Several factors combined to break this social isolation and move Cajuns toward Americanization and assimilation. The two world wars drew large numbers of Cajuns out of southwest Louisiana and into the armed forces, and the nationalistic sentiments accompanying U.S. involvement pressured them to conform. Teddy Roosevelt spoke for many when he said that in America there was "room for but one language in this country and that is the English language, for we must assure that the crucible produces Americans and not some random dwellers in a polyglot boardinghouse" (Ancelet 1989, 27). In the early twentieth century the developing oil industry lured locals away from established livelihoods, primarily as farmers, into a mainstream economy. Radio and television brought new images and messages, in English. Finally, in 1916 the Louisiana state legislature mandated public education and, five years later, public education in English. Schoolchildren were punished for speaking French on the school grounds.

The ethnic stigma long attached to Cajun identity also pressured them toward assimilation. This stigma originated in the colonial elitist view of Acadians as crass and uncultured peasants, and their worsening economic fortunes in the nineteenth century reinforced this perception. National magazine articles also tended to portray Cajuns in unfavorable ways.[9] By the middle of the twentieth century, the term *Cajun* had assumed a pejorative meaning akin to "white trash." Some Cajuns internalized negative perceptions of themselves and their culture and some, especially the small population of upper- and upper-middle-class Cajuns, participated in attempts to destroy francophone culture and force assimilation into Anglo America. Many Cajuns suppressed their francophone identity in encounters with strangers to avoid reinforcing this sense of shame or foreclosing social and economic opportunities. At best, Cajun identity was increasingly reserved for private and social life among other Cajuns; at worst, it was actively discouraged.[10]

Under pressure to assimilate and to shed a stigmatized identity, and responding to the growing popularity of music viewed as more distinctively American, Cajun musicians began integrating new sounds into their music in the 1930s and 1940s. The accordion disappeared entirely from recordings during those decades as many Cajun musicians turned to western swing, string band music, and bluegrass for inspiration. New bands appeared, with names such as the Sundown Playboys and the Hackberry Ramblers, emulating nationally popular musicians such as Bob Wills and the Texas Playboys. More songs appeared in English or mixed French and English. After years of Americanization, Cajun music seemed in danger of disappearing. Then Iry LeJeune, who cited the influence of Amédée Ardoin, brought Cajun music back to partial and temporary popularity with his recordings of "La valse du pont d'amour" [the love bridge waltz] (1948) and "La branche du mûrier" [the branch of the mulberry tree] (1949). These songs were unexpected hits, favored especially by returning soldiers nostalgic for the sounds they associated with older, more peaceful times. Other songs, such as LeJeune's "J'ai été au bal" [I went to the dance], highlighted the continued social importance of the dance hall in Cajun life.

Lawrence Walker, Austin Pitre, and Nathan Abshire began performing and recording traditional Cajun music again. Although these musicians are sometimes credited with keeping authentic Cajun music alive, their efforts were largely swamped by pressure from rock and roll, country-and-western, and pop. Many Cajun musicians turned to swamp pop, a unique blend of Cajun, country-and-western, and pop music produced by prominent musicians such as Vin Bruce, Jimmy C. Williams, and Johnny Allan. Under pressure from these Americanizing influences, so-called traditional Cajun music remained in the background, reserved for back-porch jam sessions, house parties, and some local dances.

In sum, Cajun music has long reflected and (re)-created Cajun identity and community. By (re)-creating and sustaining a common identity in the form of shared memories, beliefs, language, traditions, and social customs, Cajun music contributed to the survival of Cajuns as a distinct people. While Cajun music played a role of social cement in helping hold Cajuns together, it nevertheless only partly succeeded at countering the social and political forces pulling them apart. Despite music and other cultural expressions that helped define Cajuns as a distinct people, they continued drifting toward assimilation. Cajun music both reflected this drift toward assimilation and contributed to it. By the mid-twentieth century, Cajun culture appeared to be well on its way to extinction.

Toward Political Community

By awakening others to the beauty and value of Cajun music and culture and promoting awareness of shared interests in reversing assimilation, overcoming ethnic stigma, and countering economic marginalization, Cajun musicians helped develop a political community capable of successful collective action. They asserted their pride in Cajun music and culture, affirmed distinctive cultural ties to France and Nova Scotia, promoted cross-generational awareness of their history, and educated Cajuns about the danger of cultural extinction—efforts that led to a national and international Cajun cultural revival. Even though many people, even Cajuns, considered Cajun music raucous and raw, musicians led this revival. By affirming the value of their music without apology, they indirectly affirmed the community and culture from which it sprang.

Although the foundations for the revival were laid by the persistent efforts of musicians, record producers, and other cultural workers in southwest Louisiana, the spark that actually ignited the revival came from outside Louisiana. In 1964, the Newport (Rhode Island) Folk

Foundation decided to feature traditional sounds as well as nationally popular performers such as Bob Dylan and Joan Baez at that year's Newport Folk Festival. The foundation invited Gladius Thibodeaux, Louis LeJeune, and Dewey Balfa to perform. The Opelousas, Louisiana, *Daily World* responded with an editorial titled "They Call That Music??!!" which compared Cajun music to "cats fighting in an alley" and ridiculed the efforts of festival talent scouts to find acts in southwest Louisiana (Kedinger 1986). The task of overturning years of stigma proved formidable. Skepticism ran deep, as illustrated by another editorial in the *Daily World* (October 20, 1965), by Burton Grindstaff:

> Cajuns brought some mighty fine things down from Nova Scotia with them, including their jolly selves, but their so-called music is one thing I wish they hadn't. The first time my sensitive ears were shattered by the dissonant squall of a Cajun musician was in Eunice back in 1946. I was told that an acquaintance of mine, a fellow who seemed to be normal in other respects, was going to play an accordion "Cajun style" at some kind of local program. I was foolish enough to look forward to the event, and even to think I might be in on the discovery of something great that had been hidden from the rest of the country all these years. I broke through a window after the first stanza, went home and doused my head in a bucket of water to drown out the sound.

Grindstaff went on to connect the fate of Cajun music to the fate of Cajun culture and people: "All we can do is sit back and wait for the verdict from Newport, scared stiff. I am not sure Cajun music is on trial in Newport. It may be us. Their verdict could subject us to tortures like the world has never known before."

Friends of Thibodeaux, LeJeune, and Balfa warned them that they were being set up for ridicule. On the contrary, the audience of 17,000 at Newport responded enthusiastically. This response impressed all three musicians, especially Balfa, who returned to Louisiana determined to awaken Cajuns to the beauty of their own music and to rekindle interest in it. Balfa, who had never before played for an audience larger than two hundred, later said that "a lot of people don't realize that they have good cornbread on the table until somebody else tells them that they have one" (Ancelet 1981, 83).

Other Cajun musicians returned from festival experiences similarly impressed with their reception. For Michael Doucet, an invitation to play at a festival in France in 1974 changed his life: "It was our first experience playing outside of Louisiana. It was great. First of all, they understood the language and second, they looked to us and other Cajun musicians as being the new arm of creative French folk songs" (Dufilho 1986). Doucet embarked on a mission "to save the music of his ancestors and to protect it from commercialization" (Dufilho 1986). After participating in the Chicago Folk Festival in 1974, Octa Clark and Hector Duhon were "surprised to find that people outside Louisiana cared so much about Cajun music" (Spitzer 1982).

For some budding activists, exile rejuvenated their interest in and commitment to Cajun music and culture. In 1973 Barry Jean Ancelet had his awakening while working on his doctorate in France. At a time when he felt that "something was missing," he encountered Roger Mason playing Cajun music at a local club: "The music washed over me like a warm tide. This was what was missing. . . . That night, Cajun music was the most comforting sound I had heard in a year" (Ancelet 1992c, 11). Returning to southwest Louisiana, Ancelet visited Dewey Balfa, who encouraged him to begin documenting the music before it was too late.

Although most Cajun musicians continued to emphasize traditional songs in their repertoire, many new compositions appeared that both reflected and promoted Cajuns' critical awakening to the beauty and value of their culture. Typical of these original lyrics were Bruce Daigrepont's compositions, including "Two-step de Marksville," describing the founding of his family's hometown, and "Disco and Fais Do-Do," in which he rues his loss of cultural and ethnic roots:

I used to change the station
when I heard the Cajun songs.
I wanted to listen to the same music
as other Americans.
Now I long for the old Cajuns.
I play their records often.[11]

These expressions of cultural pride helped younger generations overcome their wariness about the culture.

For some musicians, such as Ivy Dugas, Zachary Richard, and the Balfa Brothers, asserting cultural pride meant affirming the roots of Cajun identity in France and Acadia. In his "Valse de l'heritage" [heritage waltz], Dugas refers to the Acadian exile, popularized in the story of Evangeline, and praises Cajun culture:

On the island in the bay,
They arrived on boats.
According to the story of Evangeline. . . .
The eating is good,
And religion is so strong.
I was Cajun when I was born
And I will be Cajun when I die.[12]

These musicians who were active during the Cajun revival helped popularize a certain view of Cajun history and identity rooted initially in France and Acadia but firmly planted in contemporary southwestern Louisiana as an amalgam of various cultural, ethnic, and racial influences. Recalling Cajun rootedness in France and Acadia served to identify and emphasize them as focal points of origin.

In the context of the Cajun revival, the songs just noted played a dual role of generating an awareness of problems to be solved—cultural loss and ethnic stigma—while serving as a form of political action to address the problems by preserving cultural memories and asserting cultural pride. Daigrepont, Dugas, Richard, and others expressed in their lyrics their rediscovery and reaffirmation of the value of their cultural roots and their determination to retain them. They made a virtue of Cajuns' distinctiveness. In doing so, these songs challenged the assimilationist process that required forgetting a distinctive past and shedding a distinctive identity. They helped overcome stereotypes of Cajuns as white trash and encouraged a cross-generational pride in Cajun culture and heritage by celebrating Cajun history and culture. Finally, they helped nurture a critical awareness of Cajuns as a distinct people with a shared interest in cultural survival and shedding an ethnic stigma.

Cajun musicians also helped popularize Cajun identity and culture beyond southwestern Louisiana and, in doing so, provided evidence to other Cajuns of the beauty and value of their identity and culture as perceived by outsiders. They promoted a different, more favorable, view of Cajun history, culture, and identity than many had encountered and internalized. Cajun musicians helped Cajuns achieve a critical awareness of a forgotten and distorted history and helped break through stereotypes surrounding views of Cajun identity and culture. They helped Cajuns see themselves and their lives in new ways.

Local and regional record producers such as J. D. Miller of Crowley and Floyd Soileau of Ville Platte helped fuel the resurgence of interest in Cajun music.[13] Their work made the music available beyond live performances in homes, dance halls, bars, and restaurants and opened a broader audience of both Cajuns and non-Cajuns. They also promoted greater access to recording facilities than otherwise would have been possible. The success of some of these recordings encouraged attention from larger record companies, including Arhoolie, Rounder, and Folkways, that were instrumental in bringing the music to national and international audiences.

In short, musicians helped transform Cajun communities into *a* Cajun political community with a shared awareness of mutual problems and a commitment to addressing them. Basic constituents of the community included better cross-generational awareness of history and heritage; a greater awareness of shared membership in a social group with common cultural traits and political interests; greater pride in and commitment to remaining Cajun; and more widespread agreement on minimal but key common interests, including cultural survival, eliminating the ethnic stigma attached to Cajun identity, maintaining and increasing politicians' support for Cajun culture, and promoting tourism. This community existed primarily in southwest Louisiana but had firm attachments to France and Nova Scotia and included members displaced to other parts of the United States and the world. Its membership was composed primarily of rural and lower- to middle-class people living in the small towns, bayous, and prairies of southwest Louisiana but also included some upper-class people and residents of Lafayette.

Collaborative Problem Solving

One could argue that the confrontational form of acting in concert captures this process of community formation and cultural revival. The actions of Cajun musicians and other activists could be posed in terms of resistance to assimilation and opposition to cultural imperialism and oppression by the dominant Anglo culture. Not only does this interpretation have much appeal, but it is partially accurate: many Cajuns are resisting cultural assimilation in forthright ways. Nevertheless, the pragmatic form of acting in concert better captures both the salient features of the process and Cajuns' own understandings of the revival. Only in rare instances does one encounter the explicit language and practices characteristic of resistance and opposition. In his "Réveille" [awaken] (1974), Zachary Richard excoriated "the goddamn British" who forced Acadians into exile and exhorted his listeners to awaken to the threat of cultural assimilation:

> Awaken! Awaken! the goddamn British are coming
> to burn the fields.
> Awaken! Awaken! men of Acadia,
> to save the village. . . .
> the blood of my family has watered Acadia.
> And now those damned British come
> to run us off likė cattle,
> . . . Awaken, men of Acadia
> to save our heritage.[14]

Richard's lyrics reveal a more confrontational political orientation than most Cajun lyrics. They also suggest a conscious attempt to politicize Cajun communities and galvanize Cajuns into action. In interviews, he admitted as much, saying that he intended "to shock the sensibilities" of Cajuns to "make them suddenly aware" of their politicized history and of the need to take steps to save their culture from extinction (Ancelet 1984, 98). Accustomed to treating music as a stimulus to good times, most Cajuns were not especially receptive to this militant activism, and many "wondered why Eddie Richard's boy was so mad" (Ancelet 1992a, xv). In other words, although occasionally a musician would attempt to stimulate confrontational forms of acting in concert, his audience members were not necessarily interested in participating.

Another political statement, slightly tinged with the sympathies characteristic of a confrontational form of acting in concert but nevertheless more palatable to the average Cajun, appeared on the first long-play recording (Swallow Records 1977) of Beausoleil, a band named after Joseph Broussard *dit* Beausoleil, an Acadian who led resistance to the British and later headed one of the expeditions to Louisiana:

> Beausoleil—the host of the Cajun ideal.
> It manifested itself in the form
> of a man in Old Acadie
> who faced the injustice
> of the British exile and launched
> a futile retaliation just because.
> It manifested itself early
> in Louisiana in the form
> of a man who faced
> the incredible task of relocating
> and reestablishing a society
> and founded a town just because.
> It manifests itself again in the form
> of a group of friends who face
> the eminent degeneration
> of Acadian Culture and
> play their music just because.

This inscription on the album jacket extols the attempts of Joseph *dit* Beausoleil to resist the British imposition of exile; and, by extension, the band connects his efforts to the contemporary Cajun ideal of cultural survival, which members seem to understand in similar terms of resistance. The liner notes reveal that the band intends to pursue this project of resistance by playing music and recording the history of Cajuns to connect present life in Louisiana to its French beginnings. The songs on the recording were chosen to "carry the story of our Cajun people from their Medieval-France beginnings to 'la bonne vie' in present day Southwest Louisiana" and include, for example, a twelfth-century hymn from northern France and a *contre danse* from nineteenth-century Acadia.

While there are only isolated examples of a confrontational form of acting in concert, there are many cases of collaborative problem solving characteristic of a pragmatic form. Many involve collaboration among musicians, cultural boosters, civic groups and leaders, and various levels of government. Each is based on the recognition of a set of problems to be solved—notably cultural survival, ethnic stigma, and economic marginalization—through collaborative efforts among various individuals and groups. Specific steps have included the organization of music concerts, festivals, workshops, and contests; the establishment of collaborative relationships with government agencies and units of government; and the development of educational and apprenticeship programs.

Soon after Balfa's appearance at the 1964 Newport Folk Festival, he and other activists, some of them associated with the Louisiana Folk Foundation (formed in 1965 with help from the Newport Foundation), began sponsoring traditional music contests with cash prizes. These took place at local festivals such as the Abbeville Dairy Festival, the Opelousas Yambilee, and the Crowley Rice Festival. Additional money was committed to recording Cajun musicians. Such steps encouraged musicians to dust off their instruments and begin playing publicly again.

One of the largest annual music festivals, the Festival de Musique Acadienne, began in 1974 as the first Tribute to Cajun Music. The history of this event reveals some of the challenges of cultural revival and the collaborative relationships developed to fuel it. In 1968, recognizing the value of francophone culture in southwest Louisiana, the legislature formed a new state agency called Conseil pour le Développement du Français en Louisiane [council for the development of French in Louisiana] (CODOFIL). James Domengeaux, the first director, embarked on a singular mission of teaching the French language. Because he (like many others) believed that no Cajuns had the appropriate training necessary for teaching French, and because he viewed Cajun French as degraded, Domengeaux imported French teachers from Belgium and France. Many of these teachers signed onto the CODOFIL program to avoid conscription in their own countries, and many felt culturally superior, hated Louisiana, and wanted to leave as soon as possible. In retrospect, the decision to import teachers, combined with their negative attitudes, reinforced perceptions of the backwardness of Cajun culture and angered many Cajuns, who felt that once again their culture was being insulted. In short, the CODOFIL French language program began on shaky foundations.

Toward the end of 1973, Dewey Balfa and Barry Ancelet encouraged

Domengeaux to inject some life into his struggling French language movement by helping produce a music festival. Coincidentally, CODOFIL had already agreed to host an international conference of French-speaking journalists in March 1974, and Domengeaux wanted something to show them. Although he was initially reluctant to dilute his linguistic mission, he finally agreed. Beginning with low expectations, the organizers planned to hold the event in the student union of the University of Southwestern Louisiana in Lafayette, with a seating capacity of several hundred; but growing enthusiasm about their plans led them to make several site changes, culminating in the booking of the largest available performance hall.

The first Tribute to Cajun Music took place on March 26, 1974, at Blackham Coliseum in Lafayette. The 8,000 seats inside were full, and 4,000 more people listened outside in torrential rain. The size of the crowd surprised everyone. The organizers had designed the tribute to tell the history of Cajun music. On stage that night were Inez Catalon and Marcus Landry performing a capella songs originating in France; Dennis McGee and Sady Courville performing the twin fiddle style popular before the dominance of the accordion; the Balfa Brothers showcasing the family-oriented foundations of Cajun music; Marc Savoy, Lionel Leleux, Varise Connor, and Don Montoucet performing early accordion-based dance music; Nathan Abshire with his Pine Grove Boys performing in the style of Iry LeJeune after World War II; Blackie Forestier and his Cajun Aces performing contemporary sounds; the Ardoin Family Band, featuring "Bois-sec" Ardoin and Canray Fontenot, performing early black Creole music; Clifton Chenier performing contemporary black Creole music (zydeco); and Jimmy Newman performing swamp pop. The 150 French-speaking journalists from around the world witnessed an event that organizers had hardly dared to hope for, and reports and articles sped the international diffusion of Cajun music.[15]

One indication of cultural and communal vitality is the extent to which younger generations continue to build on the traditions of their parents and older friends and relatives. The youngest musician on stage at the first Tribute to Cajun Music was Marc Savoy, age thirty-four, and most of the performers were considerably older. This signaled a problem and sounded a warning.

The tribute also revealed a gender imbalance. Historically, Acadian and Cajun women participated in music as a capella singers of ballads, primarily in private settings such as homes. Public appearances were rare. Still, this role was important because much of Cajun history and many of the connections between life in Louisiana and life in Nova Scotia and France were maintained in these traditional ballads. The first woman to perform prominently in public was Cléoma Falcon, who, with her husband Joe Falcon, recorded the popular "Allons à Lafayette" in 1928. She played the guitar and wrote many of the approximately sixty-four songs that the duo recorded over the years. But Cléoma Falcon was an anomaly. Men wrote and performed the vast majority of songs, and women rarely played musical instruments in public. The lyrics of Cajun music strongly reflect this separation of roles. Probably the most common theme is love, especially spoiled, unrequited, or broken love, composed and sung from a man's point of view. Many songs accuse women of two-timing, mean-spiritedness, and similar intentions or actions. The classic "Jolie blonde," one of the best-known Cajun tunes of all time, epitomizes this theme:

> Pretty blond, so look what you did,
> You left me to go,
> To go off with another than me,
> What hope and what future am I gonna' have?[16]

Occasionally, contemporary women musicians remedy this gender bias by slightly altering the lyrics of older songs to reflect a woman's point of view.

Apprentice programs were established to begin addressing the generational discontinuity and to reknit some of the frayed cultural connections between older and younger Cajuns. For example, Nathan Abshire took on several accordion apprentices, while Michael Doucet apprenticed himself to some of the most prominent Cajun fiddlers still alive. Fiddle, accordion, ballad, and other musical workshops were established at local festivals. Dewey Balfa won a "Folk Artists in the Schools" grant in 1977 from the National Endowment for the Arts, the Southern Folk Revival Project, and the Acadiana Arts Council to present discussions and demonstrations about Cajun music in classrooms in southwest Louisiana. By 1978, the Tribute to Cajun Music, which had become an annual event, included eight (out of a total of twenty-two) groups whose musicians were all under the age of thirty, while two of the groups were composed entirely of musicians under twenty.

Led by activists such as Dewey Balfa, Barry Ancelet, and Michael Doucet, Cajun music continued to increase in visibility and popularity at local, national, and international levels. In 1976 Doucet's band Beausoleil was invited to France, where members received medals from President Valéry Giscard d'Estaing and paraded down the Champs-Elysées in horse-drawn carriages. During the early and mid-1970s, Cajun bands such as the Balfa Brothers and D. L. Menard and the Louisiana Aces began touring extensively, spreading Cajun music and culture throughout the United States and other parts of the world, and returning to southwest Louisiana with new outlooks and experiences, including an increased respect for Cajun music and culture induced by the enthusiasm of their audiences. In particular, Cajun musicians were eager to reaffirm cultural ties with France and other regions and countries with French cultural influence, organizing tours and making efforts through their music to connect with these regions. Like the tours, music festivals were sometimes designed to affirm cultural ties and make connections between disparate people.[17]

Cajun musicians and groups began to receive regular invitations to play at eminent cultural venues such as Carnegie Hall in New York and at presidential inaugurals and other prestigious events locally, nationally, and internationally. In 1982, Dewey Balfa became one of the first recipients of a National Heritage Fellowship, sponsored by the National Endowment for the Arts Folk Arts Program. Nationally, the revival solidified its prominence with Beausoleil's 1984 appearance on American Public Radio's "A Prairie Home Companion." Two years later, the 1986 Grammy nominations in the folk and ethnic category were swept by Louisiana musicians, including Beausoleil and Dewey Balfa.[18] This acclaim also brought local fame to the musicians, making them "cultural heroes" (Ancelet 1981, 83), which was very important in rekindling young people's interest in Cajun music and culture and encouraging them to begin playing Cajun music.

Another illustration of collaborative attempts to promote cultural vitality is the "Rendez-vous des Cajuns," a Grand Old Opry–like program established in the late 1980s by local activists, the city of Eunice, and the Jean Lafitte National Historical Park and Preserve of the U.S.

Department of the Interior. A popular music and variety show presented mostly in French, the "Rendez-vous" is broadcast live over several radio stations in southwest Louisiana and is frequently hailed as a Cajun version of "A Prairie Home Companion." The program is produced "by and for local people" in order to "dispel the negative, ill-informed stereotypes which often are propagated by mainstream mass media" (Sandmel 1992, 62), and it provides both entertainment and education. In 1993 Ann Savoy and Barry Ancelet, the producer and the host, respectively, viewed the show as an opportunity to educate listeners about the breadth and beauty of Cajun culture. According to Ancelet, "I like getting the opportunity to sneak in some education along with entertainment. I call it 'guerrilla' academics" (Sandmel 1992, 62). Ancelet typically informs the audience of song sources, meaning, and significance. His commentary, along with presentations by the performers, tells listeners about their own and others' histories, reinforces collective memories, and encourages respect for Cajun culture. Savoy is sometimes criticized for booking older balladeers and other musicians who have more historical than aesthetic value. She insists, however, that the mission of the "Rendez-vous" includes the crucial task of preserving Cajun history (Sandmel 1992, 73).

Other types of governmental support for Cajun music and culture include occasional sponsorship of Cajun recordings, funding for heritage centers and theme parks that showcase Cajun and black Creole music, and various policies and resolutions designed to promote Cajun tourism.[19] Music and culture are also supported by civic organizations such as the Lafayette Chamber of Commerce, which sponsors or co-sponsors events such as the Festival de Musique Acadienne and Downtown Alive!, and local industry, which helps fund and promote cultural projects such as the Lafayette heritage theme parks.[20] The motivation of these organizations is both economic and cultural.

How effective are these pragmatic forms of acting in concert? Although Cajuns still face multiple assimilation pressures, their distinctive culture today appears relatively durable and unlikely to disappear in the near future.[21] For example, young people have become noticeably more interested in Cajun music. At some places, such as remote D.I.'s Restaurant in Basile, where a crowd including infants, teens, younger, and older adults participates in regular Friday and Saturday night dances, evidence points toward a healthy, cross-generational interest in the music. The presence of younger performers is also noteworthy.[22] Local music festivals are extremely popular. The Festival de Musique Acadienne is now held outdoors in Gerard Park in Lafayette to accommodate the more than 40,000 fans who attend each year. Many are outsiders who have come to Louisiana to experience a bit of Cajun culture, but many are also locals. A large number of everyday venues, such as dance halls, bars, and restaurants, feature Cajun music and dance; and a number of them operate year round, even during off-peak tourist seasons. Nearly every little community in southwest Louisiana has at least one dance hall, and many have several.[23] Cajun music is easier to find on the radio today than it was thirty years ago. A more indirect sign of health is the fact that approximately forty-five people now build single-row diatonic accordions in southwest Louisiana (McConnaughey 1990). Women's roles are also less rigid. Today, they perform prominently in the music scene in southwest Louisiana, and some have earned awards for their contributions to the vitality of Cajun music.[24]

Chapter 6	Stirring Up the Roux

Negotiating Cajun Identity and Relations with Black Creoles

THE DELIBERATIVE FORM of acting in concert contributes to the vitality of public life in southwest Louisiana by stimulating debate on two contemporary Cajun issues. First, Cajuns use music to debate their identity and some of their commitments. Today, much of this debate swirls around the relative merits of cultural preservation versus change. At stake is what it means to be a Cajun and the identity of Cajun culture as a whole. Second, Cajuns use music to negotiate their relations with black Creoles. Historically, music has bridged the two groups by allowing them to share experiences in a context of segregation. To some degree, this role continues as musicians from each tradition borrow freely from each other. Since the early 1980s, however, music has fueled conflict between Cajuns and black Creoles that increases and reinforces the divisions between them. Many black Creoles believe that the Cajun revival, led prominently by musicians, is a bid for cultural domination involving an incorporation of black Creole cultural expressions, including zydeco.

Debating Cajun Identity and Commitments

"Cajun music is really big [in Mamou]. That's all there is around here." So said a diner at Jeff's Restaurant in Mamou, in the heart of Cajun country, in October 1993. The other half-dozen diners in the restaurant, all of whom were participating in the conversation with the lone "tour-ist," nodded in agreement.[1]

The diner's apparently sincere avowal rose above the country-and-western music on the restaurant's jukebox. Later that night, Mamou's Purple Door Disco left its front door open so that rock and roll, disco, pop, and country-and-western could blare into the streets. Other local bars featured country-and-western music on the jukebox. Not a single note of Cajun music, live or recorded, could be heard along Mamou's main street or in its six or so taverns and restaurants that Friday night.

Despite the increased interest in Cajun music in southwest Louisi-ana, pop, rock, and country-and-western are still the most popular, judg-ing from the consumption patterns of the residents. Although Cajun music can be found across the radio dial, its presence is generally lim-ited to short programs in the early morning and on weekends. The vast majority of radio music remains rock, pop, and country-and-western.[2] The same can be said for music played on jukeboxes throughout the region. It is also clear that, despite some gains among young people, interest in Cajun music remains skewed toward older generations.[3]

Is Cajun culture thriving, as some claim? Or does it continue to approach assimilation, as others insist? The answer hinges on what is meant by Cajun culture, and the focal point of this question is the is-sue of preservation versus change. On the one hand, those who believe in preservation of a traditional Cajun culture object to the introduc-tion of certain new elements and decry the gradual move away from traditional bases. They believe that a traditional, authentic Cajun cul-ture can be identified and that it should be maintained more or less intact. Implicit in this view is the fear that cultural change means as-similation or another form of cultural death. Preservationists argue that the Cajun revival has failed to reverse the assimilation processes at work in southwest Louisiana. On the other hand, some people argue that Cajun culture has survived by adapting and accommodating to its so-cial and cultural environment and by incorporating new elements that increase its resiliency and vitality. For them, change is not simply a re-ality but a necessity for survival. Much of this debate on Cajun iden-tity is occurring because of, and through, Cajun musical practices.

Prominent among the preservationists are Marc and Ann Savoy, co-owners of the Savoy Music Center outside Eunice, Louisiana. Marc

Savoy insists that Cajun culture is "quickly changing," and he regrets it. He believes that the success of the Cajun revival has been exaggerated by "academics" who "tend to romanticize the culture too much" (Shelton 1982, 8D). According to Savoy:

> Our culture is a wonderful culture. It's simply the best because it's ours. It came from the past. We have to make sure that when the next generation comes along, we can give it to them as it was when we got it. We've got to make war on these things that are undermining our wonderful Cajun culture. . . . Cajun music is like the Stradivarius fiddle. It hasn't changed, and why should it change? It's perfect the way it is. People say something has to change to live. But it's the individual working within the style that changes. The style doesn't change. (Simoneaux 1992, 1B)

Objecting to the integration of country-and-western musical elements into traditional Cajun music, Ann Savoy articulates similar sentiments about innovation and change: "Cajun music is being heavily brutalized. It's been torn out, rearranged, and treated very badly. It makes me sick. It's just a nightmare to me. If they love country music so well, why don't they play that? Some of this music is just a complete insult to the culture" (Simoneaux 1992, 5B).

It should come as no surprise that the Savoy Music Center is nicknamed "the bunker." A sign inside the store states, "I don't go to work; I go to war!" Other preservationists include "Nonc" Jules Guidry, who tries to "preserve the [traditional] Cajun sound." At one point, he refused to add a drummer to his band because it would not be "truly authentic music. At the old *'bals des maisons'* there was no drummer. . . . We really try to go the traditional route, without the drums" (Tillson 1993). Another contemporary musician, Eddie LeJeune, believes that "traditional Cajun music is playing what the Cajuns played when they first came here, with the same meaning behind it" (liner notes for "Cajun Soul," Rounder, 1988).

L'Association de Musique Cadien Française de Louisiane, also known as the Cajun French Music Association (CFMA), was formed in 1984 in Eunice "to make sure Cajuns in the distant future don't get swallowed up into mainstream American culture" (Dufilho 1990, 3B).

By 1993 CFMA boasted eight chapters in southwest Louisiana and east Texas and approximately 2,000 member families. It sponsors Cajun musical events such as dances, festivals, and contests; organizes local dance troupes and dance contests; provides French language and dance lessons; and sponsors a variety of social events such as potlucks, family nights, and bus trips. Some chapters have scholarships for language, music, and cultural studies. CFMA publicizes the activities of its member musicians and lists of Cajun resources such as radio programs and upcoming events. It promotes members' social activism in events such as the Baton Rouge chapter's Annual Muscular Dystrophy *Fais Do-Do*, blood drives, and church fundraisers. CFMA places a strong emphasis on families and on children and teenagers. Its dance troupes include children, and most chapters actively promote education through apprenticeship programs and youth performing groups.

To preserve Cajun music and culture, CFMA attempts to influence the decisions of musicians. For example, since 1989, it has presented Le Cajun Music Awards, which in addition to honoring the contributions of musicians, influences those who are interested in being considered for the awards: innovators are less likely than traditionalists to be recognized. When deciding who qualifies for status as a Cajun musician or band, CFMA applies criteria such as whether or not the music is sung in French and whether or not the band has a fiddler. Similarly, in CFMA-sponsored dance contests, the association decides which dance steps are allowable. In one controversial decision, CFMA banned the popular Cajun jitterbug from the contests on the grounds that it is not traditional. A relative newcomer to Cajun culture, the Cajun jitterbug was invented by non-Cajun folk dancers from New Orleans, who regularly drove to Mulate's Restaurant in Breaux Bridge near Lafayette to dine and dance to Cajun music. The dance caught on among Cajuns and has supplanted the waltz and the two-step in popularity among younger dancers.[4] Although CFMA is correct in declaring the Cajun jitterbug a recent innovation, the association's position on the form's validity is vulnerable to criticism. If we examine Cajun history, we can see that dance forms have been regularly transformed, added, and dropped and that any attempt to define a traditional Cajun dance form requires a dubious assertion of preeminence for a particular time period. As recently as the late nineteenth century, Cajuns danced quadrilles, minuets, waltzes, polkas, and mazurkas; of these, only the waltz survives today. The Cajun two-step was added later, probably imported from Texas during the Texas swing era in the early twentieth century.

Prominent on the side of cultural change and adaptation is Barry Ancelet, who believes that change *is* the tradition of Cajun music: "Cajun music is very much an ongoing process. It's constantly changing, being reinvented and redefined by people who play it, in response to people who listen and dance to it. It's a process rather than a product. The change is a sign of its life" (Simoneaux 1992, 5B). Cajuns have long created their culture by absorbing other influences. As Ancelet says, "Cajuns are constantly adapting their culture to survive in the modern world. Such change, however, is not necessarily a sign of decay, as was first thought; it may even be a sign of vitality" (Ancelet et al. 1991, xviii).

Cajun culture as an amalgam of diverse cultural influences is nowhere more evident than in the world of Cajun music. Historically, musicians have borrowed, adapted, and absorbed many different cultural influences. It is a "gumbo" assembled from elements as disparate as French folk music, American Indian chants, West Indies work songs, New Orleans jazz, Texas swing, bluegrass, country-and-western, Spanish guitar music, Anglo folk songs, 1950s rock and roll, field hollers, and pop music. This diversity appears in the work of individual Cajun musicians such as fiddler Dewey Balfa, contemporary innovator Wayne Toups, Beausoleil's Michael Doucet, and Zachary Richard, each of whom cites a variety of influences in his work.[5] How far can musicians take this assemblage of experience and sound before they stop producing music that can be called Cajun? Preservationists decry the ongoing experimentation as straying too far from authentic Cajun sounds. Implicit in their stance is the presumption that one can identify traditional, authentic Cajun music and, by extension, culture. But even Marc Savoy and Dewey Balfa, both considered traditional, play music filled with a variety of influences. In short, it is more difficult to identify an authentic Cajun sound than preservationists appear willing to admit. Yet, of course, not just any sound can be labeled Cajun.

At stake in this debate is more than which side gets to be right. As Cajun musicians borrow from other cultural, ethnic, and racial influences, they contribute to the evolution of their culture. Answering "what is Cajun music?" also answers in part the larger questions "what is Cajun culture?" and "what is a Cajun?" Thus, the efforts of groups such as CFMA to define the character and boundaries of Cajun music are attempts to define the character and boundaries of Cajun culture and identity. This may be an understandable reaction to the disorderliness of cultural change, the threat of further assimilation, and the growing phenomenon in southwest Louisiana of non-Cajuns attempting to claim Cajun status to take advantage of new cultural and economic opportunities opened up by the Cajun revival. Nevertheless, the preservationist effort ignores the extent to which contemporary Cajun identity and culture are already the results of adaptation, incorporation, and assimilation. Cajuns have managed to maintain a distinctive identity and culture, but they are not marked by purity or homogeneity of character. On the contrary, they are distinctive for their heterogeneity. They have been successful in part because their music has been a communicative tool for this process. Thus, efforts by groups such as CFMA may foreclose options for continuing development and adaptation, which, some believe, mark the enduring vitality of the culture and the people, and may also close Cajun communities to outsiders interested in participation. Finally, whatever the preservationists might like to do, their efforts face daunting challenges. Their efforts are partially undermined by the market, which rewards innovators as well as traditionalists. Although many traditionalists do sell records and win acclaim, innovators such as Michael Doucet of Beausoleil and Wayne Toups of Zydecajun are particularly successful in both. Another challenge is the difficulty of sheltering Cajun culture from external influences, especially other musical influences, which determine the extent and direction of change. Making the culture impervious to change would entail sheltering it from diverse external influences, a scenario that seems improbable in today's world.

Who gets to decide what is authentic Cajun music and culture? Not only Cajuns themselves but aficionados in cities such as Minneapolis, Seattle, Chicago, and New York regularly attend Cajun concerts, dances, and other events in their cities. Some of these events are hosted by and for displaced Louisianans who stay in touch with each other and maintain their cultural ties through Cajun music and dance. But many participants are not Cajun, nor have they ever visited Louisiana. The same dual process of preservation and invention of culture occurs at these musical and dance events as well as those in southwest Louisiana. On the one hand, some aficionados attempt to reproduce musical and dance practices exactly as they believe they exist in Louisiana. Others are more apt to play with the boundaries of Cajun identity by introducing new elements and treating the music as a flexible stimulus to innovation. While the former group may be susceptible to charges of romanticization, the latter may be charged with diluting or reinventing the meaning of *Cajun*.

The many tourists who come to southwestern Louisiana seeking an authentic Cajun experience also participate in both the preservation and evolution of Cajun music and culture. They arrive with at least some preconceived notion of what Cajun culture is like, and they expect to find it in southwestern Louisiana. Locals happily oblige in order to take advantage of the economic boost from tourism. Locals provide "authentic" Cajun experiences in restaurants, music clubs, bars, and heritage theme parks such as Lafayette's Vermillionville and Acadiana. They stage an identity for the benefit of tourists, and during off-tourist time they go about their daily routines, which may include listening to their favorite Wynona Judd, Neil Diamond, or Public Enemy recordings as well as the homegrown music that tourists expect of Cajuns. Yet tourists also fuel change as they squeeze Cajuns out of their normal routines and lure them away from traditional livelihoods such as farming and fishing in order to pursue other economic opportunities made available by tourism.[6]

How much change is appropriate to keep a culture vital and resilient without tearing it away from its historical moorings? The answer is unclear. Nevertheless, what is clear is that Cajuns are still around to debate the issue in part because of their music. Through this music, they have defined and preserved some of the core elements in their culture and adapted to new times and circumstances. On the one hand, Cajun music has preserved some of the commonalities that define Cajuns as members of a distinctive community. This endurance in the face of hostile political and social forces has required the maintenance of social bonds in the form of common memories, histories, and traditions across generations and among disparate members of the society. For example, whatever their disagreements, both innovators and preservationists agree that contemporary Cajun culture should remain anchored to its French roots.

On the other hand, a static community may be a degenerating one. Members must be able to adapt to new circumstances, reinventing the defining elements of the community and re-creating its boundaries. Music has helped Cajuns adjust to changing times by developing connections and commonalities between disparate peoples and experiences. Some musicians push the boundaries of the music by incorporating outside influences, adapting the sound to suit individual and collective fancies, and pursuing more fans and greater economic success. Others retain an older, more traditional sound. Members of the public ultimately decide what they will accept or reject, based on factors such as personal taste and belief, the market, and the promotional capabilities of individual bands and musicians.

As a deliberative form of acting in concert, music provides the people of southwest Louisiana with a communicative forum through which questions of cultural survival and adaptation can be posed and alternative answers explored. Of course, it is only a single forum among others, but for Cajuns it is a prominent one. Cajun music is a communicative forum in its own right through which Cajuns implicitly and explicitly consider the issues of cultural preservation and change, and it also goads debate in other social and public arenas. The Cajun music revival has been debated throughout the region, in arenas ranging from newspapers to informal dinner conversations. It would be difficult to live there today and not have at least a modest fluency in this critical debate about preservation and change.

Let the Good Times Unroll

The deliberative form of acting in concert also comes into play in relations between Cajuns and black Creoles, who historically have determined some of their mutual identity and relations through music. Today the two groups are negotiating several issues of importance. The most important involve cultural incorporation, ownership of cultural property, and cultural identity. Many black Creoles view the Cajun revival with suspicion and resentment, believing that it is a bid for cultural dominance in southwest Louisiana. In their eyes, the revival has succeeded in part by incorporating black Creole cultural expressions, especially zydeco, into the category of Cajun music.

Among Philip Gould's (1992) collection of photographs of Cajun and zydeco musicians and musical events is a portrait of the main street of Mamou, Louisiana, during a daytime Mardi Gras celebration. The photo, which shows a Cajun band onstage in the middle of a long view of the street, captures the celebratory emotions of several thousand revelers. Also striking is the apparent absence of a single person of color. Cajuns and black Creoles celebrate Mardi Gras separately in southwest Louisiana. During the holiday, people from a particular community travel to other members' homes to visit, gather contributions for a communal gumbo, and reaffirm the shape of the community. Unfortunately, as Gould's entire book illustrates, the shape of Cajun and black Creole communities is defined by almost complete racial segregation in social arenas. This segregation is nowhere more evident than in the world of music.[7]

Segregation is unfortunate under any circumstances but especially when we consider that Cajuns and black Creoles may have more in common than not. Their histories overlap at many points, as their contemporary identity, especially in the form of music, reflects. Like Cajun music, the roots of zydeco extend several centuries into the past and onto at least three continents. Similarly, it has responded to and absorbed many different influences, particularly French and African. But while French influence predominates in Cajun music, African predominates in zydeco. Precursors include slave music in the form of rhythmic stomping; field hollers; *jure* singers; and hand clapping accompanied by rhythm instruments such as spoons, washboards, and sticks. Musicians later absorbed "la la" music—fast French dance music with a rhythm-and-blues influence developed in southwest Louisiana during the early and mid-twentieth century. Today, zydeco also reflects Africa-inspired blues, soul, jazz, and rhythm-and-blues.[8] One-, two-, and three-row diatonic accordions were introduced in the late nineteenth and early twentieth centuries, along with the frottoir—a metal rubboard. Later, some zydeco musicians such as Clifton Chenier and Stanley "Buckwheat Zydeco" Dural replaced the diatonic accordion with the more versatile piano accordion. The fiddle played an important role in early zydeco music but has largely been dropped by contemporary musicians.

Cajun and zydeco music also drew from similar, sometimes identical, individual sources. Amédée Ardoin (accordion), Freeman Fontenot (accordion), Alphonse "Bois-sec" Ardoin (accordion), Canray Fontenot (fiddle), Claude Faulk (accordion), and Bebe Carriere (fiddle) were among the black Creole musicians who provided the foundations for zydeco. These are, of course, the same musicians often cited as important early influences on Cajun music.

Zydeco also shares with Cajun music a near-fatal encounter with American assimilationist pressures. Like Cajun music, the music of black Creoles went "back porch" without disappearing entirely. According to Stanley "Buckwheat Zydeco" Dural, "when I started playing with Chenier [in 1976], you could count all the [zydeco] accordion players in Louisiana on one hand" (Hannusch 1983). As recently as the early 1980s, there were few new faces in zydeco. Called the king of zydeco, Clifton Chenier was the most active performer and recorder between the 1950s and the 1980s. His initial regional success led to a recording contract with Arhoolie in California, beginning in 1964, which brought him national acclaim, including a Grammy in 1984 for his album *I'm Here*. The only other zydeco musician before the 1980s to achieve national attention was Alton "Rockin' Dopsie" Rubin, Sr., who recorded with popular stars such as Paul Simon and Bob Dylan as well as with his band, the Twisters.

Like Cajun music, zydeco has recently revived its fortunes, achieving a national prominence that rivals and perhaps exceeds Cajun music. Zydeco recordings routinely climb onto *Billboard*'s pop charts. In recognition of their contributions to the music of southwest Louisiana, Canray Fontenot and "Bois-sec" Ardoin received in 1986 the Smithsonian National Heritage Fellowship Award. In addition to Clifton Chenier, several zydeco musicians have won Grammy awards, including Queen Ida (1983) and Rockin' Sidney (1986). Zydeco now provides the musical background for a host of national and regional television commercials, and performers make regular appearances on television shows such as "Saturday Night Live," "Late Night with David Letterman," and the "Tonight Show." Black Creoles, both men and women,

old and young, can now earn social status among their peers by performing zydeco; and many young musicians play regularly in southwest
Louisiana.[9] Finally, the musical sensibilities and lyrical themes of Cajun
and zydeco music have much in common, reflecting similar experiences
and lives. In particular, both forms of music are dominated by poverty-
and love-inspired blues.

The historical and contemporary affinity between Cajun and zydeco
music suggests an ongoing process of mutual accommodation and sharing of experience. It also suggests that, in the past, music has contributed to the creation of social bonds across the divide of economic
competition and segregation. In southwest Louisiana, like elsewhere in
the South after the Civil War, segregationist codes mandated strict social separation between blacks and whites well into the twentieth century. Economic realities partially undermined this segregation because
poor Cajuns and black Creoles worked side by side picking cotton, working tenant farms, and doing other kinds of manual labor. Cultural practices such as music also undermined segregation. In the early 1900s,
black Creole musicians played regularly at Cajun house parties, and
Cajun musicians frequently played at black Creole dances. Certain
prominent musicians also had key bridging roles. Amédée Ardoin,
Canray Fontenot, and "Bois-sec" Ardoin have already been cited for
their contributions to both musical traditions. Dewey Balfa was noted
for his willingness to cross the rigid racial lines in southwest Louisiana
and while on tour. Clifton Chenier, popular with white and black audiences, regularly played at white clubs; and whites sometimes braved
segregation to hear him perform at black Creole clubs such as Richard's
in Lawtell and Slim's Y Ki Ki in Opelousas.

The contemporary repertoires of both Cajun music and zydeco still
reflect a lively cross-fertilization. For example, many of Amédée Ardoin's
compositions continue to circulate in Cajun music, and popular Cajun
bands such as Beausoleil and Wayne Toups's Zydecajun experiment with
zydeco rhythms and instruments such as the frottoir. Some of the most
popular zydeco bands living and playing in southwest Louisiana during
the early and mid-1990s, such as Beau Jocque's Zydeco Hi-Rollers and
Zydeco Force, use Cajun single-row diatonic accordions and perform
slow waltzes and two-steps in a style similar to that of Cajun bands.
Blacks and whites still mingle occasionally at festivals and other venues.

Festival Acadienne always includes representative black Creole musicians; and Festival Internationale de Louisiane, an annual event in downtown Lafayette that attracts crowds as large as 150,000, showcases both black and white musicians from various French-speaking parts of the world, including southwest Louisiana.[10] Nevertheless, this bridging role has always been limited, and it remains so. Although musicians have sometimes been able to cross racial barriers, non-musicians have found it more difficult. Everyday social life, especially in musical venues, remains segregated, even though workplaces and schools are desegregated.

Ironically, music may be widening the gap. Many black Creoles believe that the heavy promotion of Cajun music and culture erases black Creole contributions to the culture of southwest Louisiana. They argue that this promotion unfairly singles out Cajuns as representative of the entire region, gives Cajuns dominance among the many ethnic and racial groups living there, and involves a colonization of black Creole culture. According to Pat Watters (1993, 13–14), there is "widespread disapproval" among black Creoles about the promotion of Cajun music and culture. Although they "speak in even tones about perceived white racism and discrimination . . . voices become angry when talking about the Acadian renaissance of the last 20 years."[11]

Part of the controversy originated in good intentions. By attempting to acknowledge their cultural debts to black Creoles and honestly portray their own roots, Cajun festival organizers usually invite black Creoles to take part. The first Tribute to Cajun Music included Clifton Chenier, "Bois-sec" Ardoin, and Canray Fontenot, and subsequent festivals have followed a similar pattern.[12] As Ancelet (1992a, xviii) says, these are "steps in the right direction" because they acknowledge black Creole contributions to Cajun music and culture. Nevertheless, many black Creoles continue to feel that the acknowledgment parallels a process of incorporating black Creole cultural expressions, especially zydeco, into the Cajun category.

Evidence of this incorporation is plentiful. In addition to festivals, various publications, recordings, legislative initiatives, and other public documents and pronouncements routinely subsume black Creole contributions to regional culture under the label of Cajun. Ann Savoy's popular book on the music of southwest Louisiana is entitled *Cajun Music* even though it is also about zydeco. She says in her introduction that Cajun music is "the rubboard and the triple row accordion driving to the beat of an electric bass in a black club in a creole community" as well as fiddle and single-row diatonic accordion music (Savoy 1984, xi), and she devotes approximately one-fourth of the book to black Creole and zydeco music. Ancelet's *The Makers of Cajun Music* (1984) in reality addresses both Cajun and zydeco music.[13] Because each form is intimately tied to its community, subsuming zydeco music under the category of Cajun implicitly subsumes black Creole communities under Cajun communities and, by implication, puts Cajuns in a dominant position relative to black Creoles. Sometimes zydeco is described as the music of "black Cajuns," which makes the incorporation of black Creoles complete.[14] Finally, according to the liner notes for a recording by Queen Ida and the Bon Temps Band, "zydeco music is of Cajun origin and brought to Louisiana from French Canada by the Acadians. . . . The Creoles adopted the music and added their cultural flavor."[15] This explanation condones a primary valuation of the French contribution and a concurrent devaluation of the African influence, distorting history in the process: African influences, which hardly originated in French Canada, primarily define zydeco.

Examining the roots of the term *zydeco* reveals more about the significance of incorporation. The phrase "les haricots sont pas salés" [the snapbeans are unsalted], a reference to hard times heard on an early Clifton Chenier recording, is usually cited as the source of the term.[16] Although "hard times" may be an appropriate metaphor for this bluesy music, Chenier himself offered a different explanation. According to him, the term was already circulating when he began playing music: "See, the old people used to say 'Let's go to the zydeco,' meaning the dance. And I kept that in mind, and when I started playing music I called my music 'zydeco'" (Savoy 1984, 373). The event included a communal feast with a gumbo to which all participants contributed, as well as music and dancing, and it played a central social and celebratory role in the life of rural black Creoles.[17] These cooperative, communal, and celebratory dimensions both revealed and reshaped the characteristics of black Creole communities. Thus, calling zydeco "black Cajun" music and subsuming it under the label of Cajun involves not simply an incorporation of music but of whole communities of black Creoles.

The incorporation process sometimes appears to encompass the entire culture of southwest Louisiana. Responding to tourist interest, the state legislature designated the region "Cajun Country," as many billboards announce. The University of Southwestern Louisiana rechristened its sports teams the "Ragin' Cajuns" despite the fact that a disproportionate number of athletes are African American, and the city of Lafayette renamed its bus system, used primarily by people of color, the "Ragin' Cajun Busline." You can now buy just about anything in southwest Louisiana with a Cajun label—from McCajun fries, to Cajun fishing bait, to Cajun lingerie. Barry Ancelet (1992a, xxi) notes that "Creoles are left to wonder what happened to their contribution to the French Louisiana cultural gumbo."

Since the early 1980s, black Creoles have responded with criticism and have attempted to develop a cultural revival paralleling the Cajun one. Some people, such as Takuna El Shabazz, openly criticize Cajuns for indiscriminately incorporating black Creole cultural expressions into the category of Cajun. He and others in the Lafayette area formed the Un-Cajun Committee in 1982 to draw attention to their concerns and organize a response. El Shabazz calls the Cajun promotion "a form of white colonialism" because it involves a new form of white domination (El Shabazz 1992, 43). Although he has been attacked for reverse racism, being anti-Cajun, and attempting to stir up hatred between whites and blacks, he insists that the Un-Cajun Committee exists not to oppose or disparage Cajuns but to counter the colonization of African cultural expressions and identities and to highlight the differences between Cajuns and others in southwest Louisiana.[18]

El Shabazz and members of the Un-Cajun Committee frequently draw criticism for focusing on an inconsequential issue rather than the real issues of education, jobs, drugs, and crime that plague black Creoles in southwest Louisiana. He responds that these criticisms imply that "one has nothing to do with the other." At their heart, in his view, is that black Creoles "have no real sense of [their] own history and culture," which Cajun promotion exacerbates. Robbing black Creoles of their cultural foundations adds to the social and economic problems that plague their communities, "contributing to the self-hatred syndrome of black people in Southwest Louisiana" and "kill[ing] the desire for self-determination" (El Shabazz 1992, 43, 45).

Given the agreement among many black Creoles about the problems of cultural appropriation and a bid for dominance, and the willingness of some to adopt the language and practices of confrontation, one might expect significant evidence among zydeco musicians of a confrontational form of acting in concert. With few exceptions, this is not the case.[19] Zydeco lyrics steer clear of the issue, continuing the older, blues-inspired themes, and musicians remain largely unorganized in explicit attempts to address the problem. There are several reasons. First, zydeco, like most of Cajun music, is deeply rooted in social situations of celebration, especially dancing. It is music for "les bons temps." Zydeco musicians are reluctant to taint "the good times" by injecting anger and criticism, fearing that their audiences will abandon them if they do.

Second, zydeco musicians need to cultivate the good will of white audiences to sell them records. Moreover, whites control most of the recording and production facilities and capacities in southwest Louisiana. Like their counterparts in other professions, zydeco musicians maintain relatively harmonious social and working relationships with white people to advance their own economic interests.

Third, internal social, cultural, and economic differences divide zydeco musicians and black Creole communities and derail a united collective response. Members cannot agree on the answer to the process of cultural appropriation. Although many openly support the confrontational stance of the Un-Cajun Committee, others, including some leaders, openly reject it. In the world of music, the same kinds of disagreements that emerged in Cajun communities about the definition of Cajun music have also emerged within black Creole communities about the definition of zydeco. Some black Creoles complain, for example, about replacing the fiddle with saxophones and horns. Zydeco musicians also disagree about appropriate strategies to take in positioning themselves for promotional purposes, a disagreement exacerbated by economic competition. For instance, many have criticized "Rockin' Dopsie" Rubin, Sr., for attempting to benefit from the Cajun promotion by calling his band the Cajun Twisters and crowning himself the new king of zydeco after the death of Clifton Chenier.

Although evidence of a confrontational form of acting in concert is scarce in zydeco, there is some evidence of a pragmatic form. In addition to promoting awareness of the problem, activists in southwest Louisiana are attempting to foster a revival comparable to the Cajun one; and music provides a cornerstone, increasing awareness of shared problems among black Creoles and addressing them collaboratively. Prominent annual zydeco festivals include the Southwest Louisiana Zydeco Music Festival in Plaisance and the Zydeco Extravaganza in Lafayette's Blackham Coliseum. The Plaisance festival, organized in 1982, now attracts more than 20,000 fans each year. Organizers call it "a celebration," a "revival," a "rebirth," and a "rubberstamp" of Creole culture (Guillory et al. 1993). This and other festivals are helping to return zydeco to its original sense of a communal event and to revitalize the communities in which it is set. Black Creoles now host radio and television programs on zydeco and black Creole culture.[20] They also host their own music awards program, the Zydeco People's Choice Awards. Finally, efforts are underway to promote tourist interest in black Creole music and culture by collaborating with organizations such as the Greater New Orleans Black Tourists Commission, which links interest in New Orleans's jazz with zydeco music in southwest Louisiana.[21] Like other examples of pragmatic forms of acting in concert, these actions are oriented toward organizing community members for collaborative problem solving.

In sum, by attempting to explore honestly their roots and their contemporary cultural identity, Cajuns have been compelled to seek answers in black Creole culture. The African influence in Cajun music remains strong, as Cajuns acknowledge. One can imagine a more unfortunate alternative in which they engaged in a racist attempt to deny these African roots, but musicians show little inclination to take this route.

It is possible that the current conflict in southwest Louisiana may yield positive results. Because social segregation between whites and blacks has been an accepted fact of life for a long time, its very mundaneness may legitimize and perpetuate it. The barriers of segregation prevent progress on mutual problems such as the endemic poverty that affects many Cajuns and black Creoles alike. The conflict over music has provoked greater attention to the problems of racial segregation and forced some Cajuns and black Creoles to reexamine beliefs about appropriate relations between the two groups. An opportunity exists for forming a more comprehensive, more heterogeneous community. Achieving this goal, however, requires facing some difficult issues. Musicians are forcing these issues into the public sphere, intentionally or not.

Chapter 7   Entering the Circle

Powwow Music in Minnesota and Western Wisconsin

SINCE THE LATE 1800s, much of U.S. policy on American Indians has been designed to force their assimilation with the hope that the "Indian problem" would disappear along with indigenous identities.[1] The General Allotment Act of 1887 and the series of termination acts enacted by Congress between 1953 and 1961 were among the most disastrous of these policies. The General Allotment Act (or Dawes Act) mandated the division of reservation land into individual and family plots of up to 160 acres, which, under certain conditions, could be sold if desired. Surplus tribal lands after allotment were purchased by the U.S. government at minimal cost and opened to white settlement. The act was intended to dissolve the reservation system and tribal landholding to compel Indians to integrate into Anglo-European economic, cultural, and social relationships. Actual results included the sale of large portions of reservations to whites, creating a checkerboard of Indian-white landholding within reservations. In some cases, the majority of reservation land became white-owned. For example, by 1966, only 19 percent of Minnesota's Leech Lake Reservation land was still owned by Ojibwe people (Vennum 1982, 27).

After a brief hiatus (from forced assimilation) during the "Indian New Deal," House Concurrent Resolution 108 (1953) established the goal of identifying specific tribes to be removed from federal support and supervision. The intent was again to abolish reservations and open the land to taxation, end federal programs and the special ward relationship between Indians and the federal government, and further force the assimilation of Indians. Between 1954 and 1961, Congress enacted laws on a tribe by tribe basis to terminate tribes judged administratively and economically capable of making the transition. Termination proved disastrous for many affected tribes, including the Menominee tribe of Wisconsin, which had to sell much of its land to pay its new taxes and meet other costs once paid by the U.S. government.

Other government actions designed to discourage indigenous identities and force assimilation included the 1884 ban on ceremonies such as the Sun Dance and the Ghost Dance and on dream and warrior societies (Huenemann 1992, 125; Heth 1992, 7). The Bureau of Indian Affairs (BIA), which in theory represented Indian interests, often discouraged indigenous social, cultural, and spiritual practices such as the powwow as a way of speeding assimilation (Parthun 1976, 38). The federal government established police forces and courts such as the Court of Indian Offenses at Minnesota's Red Lake Ojibwe Reservation, created in 1884, to "enforce rules forbidding plural marriages, dances, destruction of property following death, intoxication, liquor traffic, interference of a medicine man with the 'civilizing program,' and an Indian's leaving the reservation without permission" (Ebbott 1985, 11).

Christian missionaries and white educators joined these attempts to force assimilation. Many Indian children were sent to white-run boarding schools, severing them from their culture and inculcating them with white traditions and values. Indigenous languages and customs were typically discouraged (Ebbott 1985, 11). Even during the Indian New Deal, some Indian schoolchildren in Minnesota were forbidden to speak Ojibwe or engage in other indigenous practices (Vennum 1982, 28).

In light of these extensive efforts to eliminate indigenous identities, survival of American Indian identities and practices has been no little feat. After military options were exhausted, and with few apparent political options, Indian attempts to control their own fate were displaced to culture. Indians continued to engage in indigenous cultural practices despite official bans. The reservation system, which produced forced enclaves, enabled this process by providing a social space where indigenous events and ceremonies such as powwows could be practiced relatively undisturbed. For those Indians displaced from the reservations to urban areas as a result of federal policies or to survive economically, cultural practices such as the powwow worked as social cement holding the people together. Although American Indians have survived and, in some ways, flourished, the costs have been high, not only in loss of land, language, tradition, and religion but also in social and psychological terms. Various studies place some indigenous populations at crisis levels for poverty, health, rates of alcoholism and suicide, and unemployment.[2]

Although many American Indians now possess considerably more economic, legal, and political clout than they did several decades ago, many continue to look for answers to contemporary challenges in indigenous and traditional cultural practices. In Minnesota and western Wisconsin, two of these answers are survival schools and Indian drum and dance groups. Several survival schools have opened in the Twin Cities area alone. They typically offer basic courses but with an indigenous spiritual and cultural emphasis as well as instruction in indigenous and traditional language, music, dance, and spirituality. Members of the American Indian Movement (AIM) opened the Minneapolis Heart of the Earth Survival School in 1972 with thirty-five students. It eventually enrolled more than two hundred students and employed a full-time music and dance instructor. St. Paul's Red Schoolhouse opened in April 1972 with, as one organizer put it, "one box of crayons, about two dozen pencils, no teachers, no bus, no hot lunches; but we did have an ol' buckskin drum, drum sticks and some good songs."[3] Other American Indian organizations such as the University of Minnesota's American Indian Learning Resource Center, the Minneapolis Indian Health Board, and the Minneapolis Peacemakers Center also sponsor drum groups and powwows. In addition to cultural survival, this emphasis on traditional and indigenous cultural expressions aims at nurturing what Martin Luther King, Jr., (1992, 93) called a sense of "somebodiness"— self-respect and self-confidence that encourage a sense of efficacy for controlling one's fate.

Not all answers come from the past, of course. As the brochure for the Minneapolis Peacemakers Center states, the "best new ways of serving the needs of American Indian youth and their families in the community *include* the old ways" (my emphasis). Survival and recovery have been encouraged by the "political resurgence" of indigenous people over the last several decades (Cornell 1988). Cornell attributes this resurgence to an increase in political resources and the emergence of a supratribal Native American or American Indian collective actor that complements and bolsters the capacity of individual tribes for political action.[4] He distinguishes between mobilization and direct political resources (Cornell 1988, 165). Mobilization resources include, for example, organization, social cohesion, leadership, and money, while direct resources include factors such as numbers of votes, guns, money, and legal skills. Each of these political resources may contribute to the political capacity of individuals and groups. In these terms, powwow music can be viewed as a mobilization resource for promoting social cohesion and the formation and maintenance of collective actors at tribal and supratribal levels. It is a direct resource because it helps these collective actors engage in political action.

Community and Diversity at a Powwow

The powwow is often cited for its importance as a constituent of tribal and Indian identity and as a unifying force in Indian life.[5] This role is especially significant in light of the diversity within and among tribes. Although others have argued this point, much can still be added to our understanding of the specific practices that foster this unifying role. One way to consider the powwow is as a communicative arena in which shared experiences help create and sustain a common ground of memory, experience, identity, and commitment out of disparate experiences and identities.

Indian tribes differ widely in tradition, custom, commitment, and interests. Multiple differences also exist within each tribe. According to one Ojibwe saying, "if you put five Ojibwe in a room together, there will be at least ten different opinions on any subject."[6] With the exception of those hosted by supratribal and intertribal organizations such as AIM or university-based American Indian centers, powwows are usually hosted by a single tribe. Nevertheless, most modern powwows are attended by members of several tribes; more than sixty tribes from the United States and Canada may be represented at a large one. Locales also vary considerably—from urban parks, to gymnasiums, to specially built outdoor powwow arenas. On some reservations, you can now find the powwow arena next to a fancy casino, vividly illustrating the blend of old and new, traditional and contemporary in present-day Indian life. A powwow usually spans several days, from Friday through Sunday. For a reservation powwow, people arrive with tents, teepees, and motor homes and set up camp around the arena. Thus, the powwow plays a gathering role, drawing Indians together into the same space where communicative interactions can take place. It is a social event that encourages scattered friends and relatives to reconnect at least once each year and an opportunity to meet new people and make new friends. The central experiences at a powwow are music and dancing, but various other social practices occur throughout the weekend, including communal feasts, organized and unorganized competitions, religious and spiritual ceremonies, giveaways, and much informal socializing.[7]

Although there are significant differences among tribes, powwow practices among tribes of Minnesota and western Wisconsin remain largely the same, which allows me a certain level of generalization. The practices that I emphasize are generic to the region. Within the powwow grounds, participants create, reinforce, and sometimes debate the commonalities that define a community. Some of the various communicative practices occur as speech, while others are nonlinguistic. Specific powwow elements that play a unifying role include the philosophy and spirituality that underlie powwow practices; the emcee; music and dance; and explicit community-affirming practices such as feasts, honoring, giveaways, and rituals of inclusion.

While contemporary powwows include many secular dimensions, they are supported by philosophical and spiritual traditions that emphasize unity and inclusiveness.[8] For example, the physical space in which communicative interactions occur, a circle, is itself rich with significance for a discussion of American Indian unity and diversity. Among Indians of Minnesota and western Wisconsin, the circle is the spiritual embodiment of all living creatures; and relations within this circle are characterized by unity, harmony, and inclusiveness. This imagery of the circle permeates the powwow. The dance arena is always set up as a circle (or an oval if the physical space will not accommodate a circle). This includes powwows held indoors in gymnasiums, auditoriums, church basements, and other square or rectangular spaces. Musical performance is organized into drum groups—groups of four to

ten drummer-singers who encircle a drum in performance. These groups
either set up in the center of the dance arena or around its perimeter.
Dancers move in a circle around the arena. Surrounding the dance arena
are seats for the audience, and around these seats are various food and
craft vendors. Each powwow is thus a material embodiment of the underlying philosophy represented by the circle, and participation in a
powwow signifies membership in the circle.

At the core of powwow experience in Minnesota and western Wisconsin is the drum, which, in American Indian philosophy of the region, symbolizes the heart of all living creatures, including indigenous
people. As some people see it, without the drum there would be no powwow and no indigenous people. In secular terms, the powwow relies on
the drum for its central activities of singing and dancing. Because the
drum is "the heartbeat of our sacred circle," and the "sacred circle" refers to an inclusive wholeness of humans and all living creatures, the
drum has a deep spiritual significance. "If ever that heartbeat should
discontinue, we are gone, everyone is gone."[9]

Of course, not everyone brings philosophical or spiritual interests
to a powwow. Although many, perhaps most, Indians can recite the spiritual meaning underlying powwow practices, it is unclear how many take
it seriously. Some Indians are concerned about an increasing secular-
ization of the powwow. But regardless of the philosophical and spiritual orientation of participants, the powwow represents for most a place
where differences can be set aside in favor of fellowship and unity. For
some, adding a philosophical dimension intensifies this commitment
to fellowship and unity.

The character of the community into which people are invited is
defined in part by its universe of interests and commitments, some of
which are articulated by the emcee. In addition to his (the vast majority of emcees are men) role of announcing the order of events and keeping the powwow moving, the emcee plays a central role in informing
participants and observers of the significance of the events and practices as they unfold and (selectively) enforcing tribal and Indian customs. Many of these explanations are directed at non-Indians and
members of other tribes, but they are also intended to remind tribal
members of the meaning of their practices. Some emcees accomplish
this through appeals to collective memory, exhorting listeners to "re-

member." Collective memory is also reinforced with articles on tribal history, dedications to prominent tribal members, and mention of central events in indigenous history such as the Battle of Wounded Knee. At other times the emcee enforces tribal customs and traditions, such as "children should not be carried in the dance arena" and "dogs are not allowed in the powwow arena unless they arrive in a cooking pot," and exhorts participants to "watch the leaders and do what they do."[10]

By publicizing the assumptions and beliefs that underlie powwow practices, the emcee reminds participants of the significance of their actions, including philosophical and spiritual dimensions, and reinforces collective memories. The articulation of shared memories reminds members and others of common histories. Of course, different emcees handle their role differently. Some simply move things along and entertain, while others explain and comment. The emcee and other featured speakers sometimes endorse particular stands on key political issues such as American Indian self-determination, sovereignty, tribal treaty rights, and the environment. This is especially true of the powwows organized by AIM, but it is often true for other powwows as well. Articulating these issues contributes to a common awareness among participants of political issues facing them at tribal and supratribal levels.

Beliefs and commitments are embedded in the music and dancing, which emphasize repetition and unison and reinforce the commitment to unity represented by the circle in which they take place. The most common rhythms are straightforward duple, with occasional "honor" beats struck on the offbeat to honor Mother Earth or a specific person, event, or idea. The musicians drum and sing entirely in unison except for the leader's brief solo introductions. One measure of the quality of performance is the extent to which the musicians achieve a tight, cohesive sound. Although some songs contain a short lyric in the indigenous language, most songs today are composed entirely or almost entirely of vocables, or nonlinguistic syllables. There are many different kinds of songs written for different dances or other purposes. Although songs vary in intent, meaning, style, and sound, the structure remains standard within each type. The "incomplete repetition" form, or AA/BCD/BCD, is the most common and, like the other song forms, is quite short.[11] Thus, for a dance, the song is repeated in "pushups" for a designated or requested number of times—usually four or five times but longer during a grand entry or for popular dances.

Drumming is associated with both aesthetic and spiritual power. Whatever the drumming might lack in complexity it makes up for in intensity of expression and reception. In his study of Menominee pow-wow music, Slotkin (1957, 14–15) refers to "the tremendous dominating drumbeat which makes everything vibrate to it. . . . I never had such a sense of rhythm penetrating me."[12] The unison singing, when done with skill and conviction, adds power and forcefulness to this shared affective experience. The net effect is a potent physical and, for some, emotional experience shared by musicians, dancers, and listeners. Pow-wow participants react in qualitatively different ways and varying degrees of intensity, but most find it hard to ignore. For people who bring spiritual interests to the powwow, the drum is also "the most important material embodiment of [spiritual] power" (Slotkin 1957, 35). Because the drum is considered the heartbeat of Mother Earth, beating on the drum puts people in touch with spiritual powers. It is a form of communication, a means of summoning strength from the spiritual world.

The intertribal dance is the most common social, noncontest dance. Anyone can participate, including non-Indians and people wearing street clothes. The step is a basic one-two, touch-step requiring only minimal expertise, but experienced dancers sometimes display their more advanced steps during an intertribal. There are several dance categories on the Northern Plains powwow circuit, each characterized by a distinct set of stylistic norms and movements. For men, these include traditional, grass, and fancy dancing; for women, traditional, jingle dress, and fancy shawl. Individual expression occurs but within the parameters of each type of dance. Despite variations in style, each dance builds on multiple repetitions of the simple one-two, touch-step that characterizes grand entries and intertribal dancing. Variations are woven around this basic step according to the artistic fancy of the dancer. During most dances, the dancers must pay close attention to the singers in order to stop dancing at the same time that the singers stop. This is especially true for contest dancing, where points are deducted or the dancer disqualified for not stopping on cue. Focusing attention is made easier by the fact that most songs have a similar structure, and musicians also include clues such as slight changes in drumming patterns.

These aesthetic qualities of repetition and unison in powwow music and dancing complement and reinforce the underlying powwow philosophy of unity and inclusiveness. They encourage concentration and intensify sharing as participants engage simultaneously (if temporarily and at varying levels) in the central practices that define the powwow.[13]

Several powwow practices explicitly and intentionally affirm and reinforce communal relations among Indians. One practice that occurs frequently at a powwow and that reinforces the implied and explicit commitments to respect and fellowship within powwow experience is the custom of honoring. Implicit forms of honoring include the grand entries—the inaugural events occurring several times during a powwow in which the dancers enter the circle to the sound of singing and drumming—which are led by honored military veterans. Many instances of honoring occur explicitly. Participants generally funnel their explicit requests to honor another relative, friend, or member of another tribe through the emcee, so it is usually done publicly and is often accompanied by a giveaway. The giveaways are themselves explicit expressions of honor and appreciation for one or more individuals. This custom of honoring plays the role of affirming and cementing social relationships among various tribal members. It is a formal means of publicly acknowledging an important social relationship and of expressing an enduring commitment to other members of the tribe and, sometimes, to members of other tribes.

Various formal and informal mechanisms are used to invite inclusion and participation in the powwow circle. For example, the emcee typically issues an invitation to join the circle—welcoming tribal members, members of visiting tribes, non-Indians, and other prominent visitors and encouraging everyone to participate. The communal feasts, to which everyone is invited, also encourage participation. Other mechanisms for inviting or signaling inclusion involve ritualized use of singing and dancing. For example, grand entries are led by military veterans, signaling to powwow participants their integration into the circle and place of honor within it. This has special significance for Vietnam veterans, for whom reintegration into U.S. life has sometimes proven difficult. Other ritualized welcomes can occur at the request of powwow participants who either wish to return to the circle themselves or want to invite or signal another's return or entrance. One such event occurred at the 1993 Prairie Island Dakota powwow. A young man who had been out of the circle for six years wished to return. Working through the emcee, he announced a special song and dance, accompanied by a give-away and a public honoring of his grandfather, to mark his return. Accompanied by two special friends, and followed by tribal elders and family members, he began dancing slowly around the arena. People from the audience entered the arena to greet him and welcome him back, then joined the dancers at the rear. As they danced, slowly increasing in number, family members spread blankets, shawls, and money around the arena, which members of the audience were free to pick up. The arena gradually filled up with tribal members dancing the young man back into the circle and with others participating in the giveaway. During this event, the emcee told the young man's story of falling away from the circle and his reasons for wishing to return, articulated the importance of this public affirmation, and encouraged everyone to "come down and welcome him back."[14]

The invitation to participate does have limits. While efforts are made to keep the powwow inclusive, participation requires some respect for and adoption of the norms of the host tribe or organization. The host tribe expects visitors to respect its customs and behave more or less in accordance with them. In addition, financial considerations underlie the commitment to welcoming and inclusion. The powwow committee often needs the gate receipts of members of other tribes and non-Indians to pay the bills, which include honorariums for dancers and singers, feasts, and prize money for contest powwows.

Powwow practices re-create and reinforce existing beliefs and commitments and foster their common possession. This process of "making common" occurs at both tribal and supratribal levels. Tribal identity is articulated through distinctively tribal commitments; frequent references to tribal memory, history, and tradition; and the reinforcement of tribal customs and styles of singing and dancing. A similar process of identification occurs across tribal boundaries through the development and reinforcement of common memories and histories and occasional references to political, social, cultural, and economic issues that span tribes. The partial consolidation of musical and dance styles, which characterizes contemporary Northern Plains powwow practice, both reflects this growth of a supratribal identity and helps create it.[15] Nevertheless, identification at a supratribal level does not replace tribal identification. Some powwow participants *only* identify with their particular tribe. For others, a supratribal identification complements their tribal identification without replacing it.

In sum, the powwow is a unifying force in American Indian life, gathering diverse Indians into an arena where communicative interactions define a common ground of identity, belief, and commitment. The practices that form the powwow—singing and dancing, feasts and giveaways, fried bread and Indian tacos—build a sense of "who we are," of what it means to be both a member of a particular tribe and an American Indian.

The Powwow As a Deliberative Forum

Thus far I have treated the powwow as an arena in which unity and social cohesion are fostered and the commonalities of community created and reinforced. But a powwow is also constituted by disagreements that provoke conflict and challenge existing beliefs and practices. These disagreements sometimes fuel explicit debate as Indians discuss among themselves the relative merits of different powwow practices. Discussion and argument occur in the arena and on the sidelines, among members of organizing committees, in informal interactions among participants, and outside the powwow grounds entirely. Some disagreements are worked out directly within powwow practice, while others are not. Sometimes the debate may occur in wordless challenges and responses to existing practices. In short, Indians do not simply reaffirm the defining characteristics of their communities; they also negotiate them. The powwow can be viewed as a public arena in which they engage in deliberative forms of acting in concert involving their identity and commitments. The outcome of these deliberations depends on power, understood to mean both domination (control of others) and capacity (possession of the abilities and resources necessary to formulate goals and bring them to fruition).

Powwow practices are gendered in ways that both reveal and reinforce relations of power between men and women. This is apparent in music and dance performance. As I have discussed, music performance is organized into drum groups. In Canadian tribes and tribes of the western and northwestern United States, women sometimes join or form drum groups; but in Minnesota and western Wisconsin women rarely participate in them. Women's roles are generally limited to "helping the men" by singing an octave above the men's voices. Day-to-day musical performance implicitly reinforces this commitment to gender exclusion. Some women have attempted to challenge the practice by forming all-women drum groups, but their efforts have met limited acceptance.[16]

A more successful attempt to challenge gender roles has occurred in powwow dancing. Traditionally, male dancing is athletic and vigorous, while female dancing is demure and restrained. But one of the most popular contemporary forms of dancing for girls and young women, fancy shawl dancing, involves spirited, athletic movements. Fancy shawl dancing is a relative newcomer to the powwow scene, introduced within the past thirty-five years by girls and young women who persisted in its practice even though many people believed that it was inconsistent with traditional expectations for women. Now it is an accepted form of dance on the Northern Plains powwow circuit.[17]

The outcome of such challenges depends on relative power. Women's attempts to redefine their status within powwow practices depends partly on the support of the emcee, who is responsible for articulating and enforcing tribal customs, a role that most emcees play selectively. The emcee is a dominant voice chosen by a dominant powwow organizing committee and may or may not fairly represent the interests and views of the entire tribe. Attempts to redefine gender relations also depend on women's ability to enlist the support of other women and men and to challenge related commitments such as the commitment to unity, which pervades powwow experience and discourages participants from raising public challenges to prevailing norms and practices.

Indians also disagree about the relative weight of secular versus spiritual concerns in powwow experience. Some fear that the powwow is being secularized, stripped of its spiritual content. One example of this disagreement concerns the use of the eagle bone whistle and similar carved whistles. These whistles are carried by select military veterans and, in traditional use, are blown during the start of spiritual ceremonies to call in the power of the spirits. Some whistle carriers, however, also use them for secular purposes during music and dance performance.

In contemporary powwow practice, a dancer with a whistle will sometimes blow it to tell members of the performing drum group to pass through the song again. Given that twenty or more drums may show up to play at a powwow, the time allotted to each one can be small. One way for dancers who have been honored as whistle carriers to prolong the play of favorites is to blow their whistles. Some powwow participants object to this secular use of the whistle, arguing that it dilutes its spiritual significance; and sometimes the emcee or a spiritual elder will interrupt the dancing to admonish the whistle carriers publicly.[18]

Another secular versus spiritual disagreement involves the growing prominence of financial concerns at powwows. As the number of powwows multiplies, there is more competition among organizing committees to attract dancers and singers. One way to lure them is to offer higher prize money and honorariums. The development of a casino economy among some Indian populations has made considerably more money available for certain powwows. Some Indians fear that these developments encourage financial incentives rather than spiritual, cultural, and political incentives for participating in powwows. Some also believe that the emphasis on contest dancing and singing introduces unhealthy competition into the dance arena, which disrupts the "good medicine" of friendship and fellowship. Contest powwows clearly disrupt traditional practices such as the giveaways, which are likely to be shunted to early morning hours, and social dancing, which must be decreased to free time for contest dancing.

A related disagreement concerns the question of which drum groups will play at a powwow. Traditionally, the powwow organizing committee simply issues a general invitation to drum groups to show up and register to play on a first-come-first-served basis, sometimes to an advertised limit of twenty or thirty groups. Some of these groups are composed of accomplished veteran musicians, others of amateurs whose performance may be well short of accomplished. In traditional practice, there is no attempt to favor groups; performance simply rotates. In hopes of assuring high-quality music and attracting more and better dancers, some organizing committees now hire one or more exceptional drum groups to play the role of host drum(s). Some powwow organizing committees further limit musical participation by designating their powwow as closed drum, meaning that only invited drums whose musical performance is assured can play. This practice is controversial because many believe that it contradicts the powwow ethics of welcoming and inclusiveness.

Indians also disagree about whether it is appropriate to politicize the powwow explicitly. Some Indians distance themselves from any political uses of the powwow or related practices such as drumming, arguing that politics is divisive and contradicts the unity that should pervade powwow experience. They also object to the emcee's (or others') introduction of political themes. In contrast, other Indians pointedly introduce political issues into the powwow and carry the powwow drum into other political arenas, such as demonstrations. This is especially true of the powwows organized by members of AIM.

The secular power of factors such as casino money plays an increasingly influential role in determining the nature of powwows. Because many Indians have been economically marginalized, it is not surprising that this secular power often overwhelms the power wielded by spiritual elders and others determined to maintain the spiritual character of powwows. Similarly, the spiritual authority of elders is sometimes overwhelmed by the wholly secular interest of many people, especially youth, in having a good time dancing to the best drum groups, whose play is prolonged by blowing a whistle. Finally, members of AIM sometimes enlist the power of the media in publicizing their political goals through powwows or powwow practices. Their success in garnering media attention inevitably encourages national audiences to associate American Indian drumming with political protest, whether or not the majority of Indians view the association as appropriate.

Disagreements over the appropriate relation between Indians and non-Indians are sometimes negotiated in and around powwow practices. While the invitation issued by the emcee to non-Indians to participate in powwow practices appears genuine, it is sometimes uncertain how to handle situations that arise such as inappropriate dancing or photographing dancers inappropriately. Although the majority of non-Indians who attend powwows may behave respectfully and appropriately, some do not. A common sight at a powwow is a non-Indian snapping photographs of dancers. This strikes some Indians, especially those for whom the powwow carries spiritual significance, as inappropriate, especially when the photographer actually gets in the way. Some Indian dancers, on the other hand, are apparently happy to oblige requests for posed photographs. Another occasional sight at some powwows is the attempt by some non-Indians to participate in the social dancing. While some fit well into the dancing, others stand out by attempting to improvise. Sometimes inappropriate behavior is studiously ignored, sometimes it is guardedly ridiculed, and sometimes the emcee or others may intervene. Indians also disagree about whether non-Indian participation should extend to drum groups. Although this issue is rare in Minnesota and western Wisconsin, it is nevertheless controversial.

Indian relations with non-Indians are also partly negotiated at powwows in discussions and debates over the best response to the appropriation of Indian culture by non-Indians. One example is the use of Indian symbols and names by sports teams. At some powwows one can observe simultaneously a representative from AIM decrying such uses and several Indian youths wearing sports caps and jackets imprinted with the offending logos. It may be tempting, on the one hand, to discount the wearing of these sports logos as the ignorance of youth or, on the other hand, to romanticize it as a defiant gesture of reappropriation. These may both be true. Another plausible interpretation, however, would simply emphasize that some Indians do not object to the use of these names by sports teams. The powwow is apparently open and flexible enough to accommodate these competing views on this issue, even when AIM is the powwow organizer. Another example of disagreement over the best response to the appropriation of Indian culture by non-Indians concerns the use by New Age spiritualists of American Indian practices such as drumming and sweat lodges. Some Indians cooperate in these appropriations for various reasons, prominently including profit and helping others gain spiritual guidance and understanding. On the other hand, others criticize these practices on grounds of cultural appropriation and theft of key identifying symbols and practices that many believe degrade and dilute their significance.

For most of these disagreements, there are no formal guidelines to serve as decision rules. Each is subject to debate and negotiation. They are worked out in various ways, ranging from mutual tolerance, to wordless acts of rebellion, to explicit forms of conflict and negotiation. Actual outcomes depend on multiple factors, such as the emcee and his mood or his inclination about a particular issue; the powwow organizing committee, which has incomplete control over powwow events; the tribe and its customs; the mix of participants; and the relative power of different participants. Outcomes also change from powwow to powwow, even within a given tribe.

Although the dual roles of the powwow—fostering unity while enabling disagreement and debate—may seem incompatible, in fact they are complementary. Enabling disagreement and debate contributes to the resiliency of Indian communities by helping manage the tension between unity and diversity. While disagreement and conflict are inevitable among diverse peoples, the powwow provides a public communicative forum where these differences can be expressed and negotiated. This is the signal of a healthy, vital community—one that has a place for working out differences without squelching or ignoring them.

Community Organizing for Collaboration

American Indians in Minnesota and western Wisconsin use musical practices in pragmatic attempts to organize communities for collaboration on shared problems. One illustration occurs annually in the Phillips neighborhood of Minneapolis, an inner-city neighborhood composed predominately of Native, African, and Asian Americans. In the 1990s, conflicts among these residents undermined attempts to address neighborhood problems, especially a surge in crime. In response, residents organized a Unity Powwow in May 1993 to promote awareness of the crime problem and build a coalition within the neighborhood to address it. Unlike other powwows, which include only American Indian music and dance, the Unity Powwow gave various cultural, ethnic, and racial groups a chance to showcase their culture and invite participation in it. Although the event primarily sought to organize residents across cultural, racial, and ethnic differences, it also worked to promote respect for other kinds of differences. For example, State Representative Karen Clark was honored for her work in passing human rights legislation on behalf of lesbians and gays.[19] Neighborhood residents, led by the group "People of Phillips," followed up the Unity Powwow with a Harmony Series of Sunday afternoon concerts. Each concert featured the music of a particular ethnic or racial group living in the neighborhood. Like the Unity Powwow, the intent of the series was to promote greater awareness of and respect for differences, both for their own sake and as a prelude to addressing shared problems and concerns.

A larger Unity Powwow was organized for May 1994 that sought to integrate the growing Hispanic population in the neighborhood by linking the powwow to the Hispanic Cinco de Mayo celebration. Held on May 7 and 8, this event promoted a "circle of nations"—an inclusive community, given the significance of the circle—and was billed as an opportunity to "deepen our understanding and practice of neighborliness and grass roots democracy." The circle hoped to "break down the barriers of ignorance and isolation" separating the different groups.[20] The Phillips powwow arena was linked to a Cinco de Mayo street celebration by a community parade and frequent buses traveling between the two sites. Once again, the event showcased not only American Indian music and dancing but those of Mexican, Norwegian, Hmong, and African Americans. The second Unity Powwow was also used as a platform to increase awareness and pride for past accomplishments in the neighborhood and erase outsiders' negative perceptions of the area. Touted were the removal of a liquor store from Peavey Park, the removal of a pornography theater from Franklin Avenue and the establishment in its place of the New Franklin Community Cultural Center, the establishment of a teen night club, called Mr. Art's Bar, and the transformation of a planned garbage transfer station into a "green institute."

Another illustration of this form of collaborative, community-based political action is the September 1991 powwow co-sponsored by AIM and several environmental groups to organize and promote a Mississippi River revival. Held in Fort Snelling State Park in Minnesota, the powwow featured music as diverse as rap, country-and-western, and folk as well as American Indian. It brought together a diverse population that organizers hoped to weld into a political community ready to battle river pollution. According to one observer, the event "affirmed healthy unions of indigenous rights groups with environmental groups. People of all races danced together appreciating their own and each others' cultures. . . . This unity is a resource of strength for everyone to continue their work promoting integrity of life on Earth" (Hopkins 1991, 19).

The organizers of these powwows worked primarily to promote awareness of and support for specific problems, to organize communities to act collectively on particular issues. Secondary, but related, goals included promoting unity in community and pride and respect for differences. Because collaboration among diverse groups is difficult when differences fracture and divide, the unifying and integrating qualities of the powwow were called upon to create and affirm ties between disparate peoples, promote mutual understanding and respect, and build capacity for recognizing common problems and acting on them.

Nevertheless, a caveat is in order. We should not exaggerate the bridging role of powwow music and the powwow in general. The casual non-Indian observer of powwow practices may be more likely to experience a sense of apartness and exoticism than learn to respect indigenous peoples. With too little understanding of the rich spiritual and aesthetic philosophy underlying powwow practices, it may prove difficult to appreciate the subtleties of powwow music and dancing. These limitations on the bridging role work both ways. When non-Indians at a powwow tread heavily on Indian customs, intentionally or not, Indian toleration of non-Indians can diminish. In short, the powwow may contribute to social cohesion and community in American Indian life, but its ability to produce a larger community of Indians and non-Indians marked by understanding, respect, and appreciation is limited by interpretive and other hurdles. This conclusion seems even more likely if we consider the incompatibility between Indian and white interests on issues such as land claims, treaty rights, and white appropriation of indigenous cultural symbols and practices.

Of course, powwow music represents only a portion, albeit a large one, of the total music produced and consumed by American Indians. Indian musicians such as John Trudell, Buffy St. Marie, R. Carlos Nekai, Joy Harjo, Keith Secola, Floyd Westerman, Paula Horne, Paul Ortega, and Buddy Red Bow are popular among Indian listening audiences.[21] These musicians, some of whom also attract non-Indian audiences, blend traditional instruments and sensibilities with mainstream instruments and performing venues. R. Carlos Nekai, whose concerts in Minneapolis and St. Paul typically sell out, is best known as a traditional flutist but also makes extensive use of synthesizer, electric guitar, electric bass, and trumpet. John Trudell, Floyd Westerman, Keith Secola, and Joy Harjo sometimes combine mainstream instruments such as guitar and saxophone with American Indian powwow drumming and singing. Their music sounds more familiar and accessible to many non-Indian listeners while introducing them to American Indian musical, cultural, and political themes. These musicians fill a crossover role, playing to both Indian and non-Indian audiences. This does not preclude social criticism, as the lyrics of Trudell, Westerman, Secola, and others demonstrate. The musicians play a role similar in many ways to that of powwow musicians and engage in many of the same political practices, using music to create, reinforce, and change Indian identities and communities. This crossover music is often used alongside the music of mainstream Euro- and African-American artists to build collaborative ties among Indians and non-Indians. At large concerts, it may work to create political ties and alliances in support of various causes. These concerts are typically organized to raise both money and consciousness, but an implicit benefit is the coalition they create between American Indians and other groups.

Powwow Music and Political Confrontation

Powwow music is often used in Minnesota and western Wisconsin to engage in confrontational forms of acting in concert. To non-Indians, these forms are the most visible ones. Their intent is partly expressive but includes enlisting sympathy and support for American Indian causes and galvanizing political participation. At a minimum, they draw attention to the concerns of American Indians.[22]

During the 1980s, white residents of northern Wisconsin faced off frequently with American Indians attempting to spearfish according to their treaty rights. The whites saw spearfishing as a threat to the tourist economy because it depleted the stock of walleyes, while the Indians wished to continue traditional practices guaranteed in treaties. A crowd of angry whites frequently formed to demonstrate against the spearfishers, while supporters of the spearfishing and of indigenous treaty rights enforcement gathered on the site in support. Occasionally, the events grew ugly, with racial taunts and jeers.[23] On the American Indian side, a drum was constantly present, summoning attention away from the taunts and jeers, focusing attention on the drum itself as an expression of spiritual power and unity, and encouraging solidarity among American Indians and their supporters. Other examples, witnessed by national television audiences, occurred during the 1991 World Series and the 1992 Superbowl, both held at the Humphrey Metrodome in Minneapolis. American Indian activists organized demonstrations outside the arena before and during the sporting events to protest the use of American Indian names and symbols as mascots—respectively, Braves and Redskins. Demonstrators at both events were led by an American Indian drum, again used to summon spiritual and aesthetic power, focus attention, and encourage solidarity.[24]

These confrontational forms of acting in concert occurred in a context of incompatible interests. Indian interest in continuing the traditional practice of spearfishing contradicted resort owners' interest in maintaining as large a stock of walleyes as possible. Similarly, Indian interest in maintaining control of cultural symbols was incompatible with the profit interests of sportswear manufacturers and advertisers and the interests of youth in appropriating symbols that give them a sense of belonging and respect among their peers. While Indians and resort owners can compromise by agreeing to a limited period of spearfishing and a limited take of walleye each year, each walleye speared by Indians nevertheless represents one less fish available for resort customers. The possibility of compromise on the issue of misappropriation of Indian cultural symbols appears even more remote: either sports teams and equipment manufacturers use Indian names and symbols as mascots, or they do not. In other words, both issues are constructed in either-or terms. Without common ground, Indians can negotiate for a resolution favorable to their interests, a strategy that they followed at length in both cases, while pursuing a strategy of resistance to the attempts of resort owners, sports teams, and equipment manufacturers to maximize their own interests at Indian expense.

	Music, Community,
Chapter 8	and Diversity

ALTHOUGH MUSIC CAN provide a communicative forum through which commonalities of community are created and developed, the examples discussed in this book also confirm that these communities will sometimes be marked by extensive conflict and that music can undermine and block community. Like other communicative vehicles, music lends itself to both integrative and disintegrative uses, either of which may have democratic outcomes. Whether music acts as social cement or social solvent depends on the specific intentions of musicians and listeners and on the specific social roles of music in a particular historical and cultural context.

The identity and political commitments of a diverse community cannot be taken for granted. In varying degrees, differences of ethnicity, race, gender, class, and political orientation create disagreements about communal identity and commitment. Do means exist for negotiating those differences and disagreements? Music can be one way of answering that question, providing a communicative arena in which differences within a community can be expressed and perhaps negotiated. Thus, music may enable the coexistence of community and diversity. In the Cajun and American Indian cases, part of music's political significance was its role in creating and maintaining commonalities of community as well as handling the demands of diversity. On the one hand, music offered a communicative forum for maintaining some of the bonds of community and ensuring the survival of a people. On the other, it provided a way of solving internal differences within the community, inviting others to participate in the life of the community, and working out relationships with others outside the community.

In none of the examples did music overcome all political differences to produce a harmonious, unified community. Unity, to the degree that it was achieved, was based on a limited number of shared interests and common commitments. Significant disagreement remained in each case. The Cajun example in particular shows that tension and conflict can play beneficial roles in increasing the vitality of public life by encouraging community awareness of key issues and goading debate and deliberation about differences.

The Chilean case was unique with respect to this question of community and diversity. New song musicians helped cement an alliance on the political left between some members of the middle, lower, and professional classes. Because the process occurred with relatively little disagreement and conflict, given the high level of commitment to democratic socialism, political figures such as Salvador Allende, and redemocratization after the coup, it muted internal class, racial, and ethnic differences that existed on the left and otherwise may have surfaced. Yet during Allende's presidency, the left began falling apart over questions of political strategy, contributing to the demise of the Popular Unity and increasing the likelihood of a coup. In other words, in contrast to the Cajun and American Indian cases, the conflict that did surface briefly on the left proved to be a factor in the demise of a collective actor.

Music may also define the borders of a community—what it means to exist both inside and outside the community—which inevitably defines a dichotomy of "us" and "them." In each example in this book, musical practices helped generate a sense of "we" in relation to others—a "they." Chileans on the political left, American Indians, and Cajuns all defined themselves in terms of their differences from others. For example, new song in Chile clearly defined a community of democratic socialists in opposition to members of the political right. Playing and listening to new song was itself a clear expression of membership in this community. For powwow music, borders between different tribes were sometimes blurred in practice, but those between Indians and non-

Indians usually remained well marked. Nevertheless, non-Indians were sometimes invited to join Indians in forming entirely new communities for political purposes. In these cases, the boundaries of community were not simply blurred but re-created. The boundaries of the Cajun community were the most indistinct of the three cases. They are subject to ongoing debate among Cajuns, and many non-Cajuns regularly engage in the musical practices that define Cajun identity and community, contributing to further blurring.

Music can bridge borders between communities but can also undermine those bridges. In Chile, for example, music played the positive role of creating some unity among democratic socialists, but with the partial exception of canto nuevo, prevented the building of bridges between the political left and right. The fact that music did not play a bridging role has more to do with the intentions of the musicians and their relation to wider political movements than with music or the nature of community. Cajun music and the often good intentions of musicians were not enough to build bridges with black Creole communities. Understanding this failure requires that we consider the various class, racial, ethnic, and cultural elements that define the enabling and limiting context in which music operates. In the Cajun case, despite partial similarities of identity, complex racial and class relationships created a situation in which music increased the gap between two communities. The examples in this book suggest that we must not underestimate the obstacles that limit the bridging role of music, including mundane problems of interpretation as well as stubborn racial, ethnic, class, gender, and political barriers.

Political Action

The deliberative form of acting in concert proved crucial to understanding the public life of Cajuns and American Indians. This deliberative form begins from a recognition of the political consequences of diversity for life within and between communities. In a truly diverse community, we can expect to find multiple differences of belief, interest, and commitment. Because disagreements will arise and challenges to existing beliefs and practices surface, debate and deliberation are necessary components of public life in a democratic community. The Cajun and American Indian examples show that this debate can occur through and because of musical practices. In both cases, music provided a communicative forum for articulating differences, examining elements that define the community, posing alternatives, initiating challenges to existing commitments and practices, and engaging in the implicit and explicit debate necessary for negotiation. Music thus increased the ability of the community to respond constructively to differences. Both cases also confirmed that musical practices sometimes serve as a communicative arena in which relations between two or more distinctive peoples are negotiated. For example, American Indians partly determine their relations to non-Indians through powwow practices; and Cajuns determine their relations to black Creoles, tourists, and other non-Cajuns through music. In Chile, while hostile relations between members of the democratic left and the political right were partly determined through music, there was little hint of the debate and discussion characteristic of a deliberative form of acting in concert. Its absence marked a serious problem, contributing to the failure of politics during the Allende presidency and opening the possibility of a military coup.

The pragmatic form of acting in concert can also be a response to the challenges of diversity. Although this form begins from the presumption of common interests, diversity magnifies the challenges of recognizing and acting on those interests. Music sometimes serves as a communicative basis for discovering and creating commonalities and acting on them. In this book, paradigmatic examples are the Phillips Unity Powwows, organized to promote unity in a community so that neighborhood residents could recognize and address common problems such as crime. These powwows involved, first, building class, ethnic, racial, and cultural alliances and collaborative relationships to promote awareness of problems that cut across the neighborhood's cleavages and, second, organizing to address those problems. The experience of residents in the Phillips neighborhood shows the long-term benefits of a pragmatic form of acting in concert: collaborative relationships may remain in place after the immediate problem is addressed. Thus, organizers were able to increase their support from the first Unity Powwow to the second and expand its reach.

Cajuns also turned to pragmatic forms of acting in concert to discover and act upon mutual interests, some of which cut across social classes and required collaboration among disparate Cajuns and between Cajuns and Anglos. These interests, which included survival of Cajun culture, removal of ethnic stigma, and promotion of economic opportunities through tourism, coexisted with competing interests. The value of the pragmatic form was its role in building an extended community of Cajuns defined by awareness of these mutual interests and a commitment to address them. Although this form of acting in concert also surfaced in the poblaciones of Santiago in efforts to organize neighborhoods around issues of youth disillusionment and alcohol and drug abuse, its absence in the larger context of Chilean national politics points again to lost opportunity. New song musicians could have attempted to build collaborative relationships linking the political left and right, but they did not.

Because diversity can generate incompatible and competing interests, members of one community sometimes pursue political agendas that conflict with the agendas of other communities. Thus emerges the confrontational form of acting in concert: the use of music to marshall the energies of one community against another. The form overwhelmingly defined the political character of Chilean new song. Most musicians viewed their role in explicitly oppositional terms even if, as in canto nuevo, the oppositional messages had to be hidden. New song musicians believed that their work was part of a larger movement of resistance to external economic and cultural intervention, to reformist and conservative elements internally, and to the repression of Pinochet. The failure of Chilean new song musicians to achieve some of their goals through the confrontational form of acting in concert does not mean that the form is an invalid approach to politics. Musicians did succeed in cementing an alliance on the political left composed of diverse social elements.

The form also surfaced among American Indians and was used relatively effectively to promote awareness of Indian political causes and enlist support for Indian causes. By contrast, the form barely appeared in the Cajun case. It is possible that a confrontational form of acting in concert would have promoted a more activist stance toward problems facing Cajuns and galvanized more organized forms of political participation in addressing them.

There are many hybrids of these three forms of acting in concert.

For example, canto poblacional musicians sometimes used their music to address problems collaboratively within local poblaciones, but the musicians often viewed their work within the larger oppositional framework of resistance to Pinochet and solidarity with nueva canción and canto nuevo. At the Cajun "Rendez-vous," musicians addressed the problems of ethnic stigma and survival as a culture while simultaneously (and often implicitly) debating the identity of their community.

Music and Political Capacity

By enabling Chileans, American Indians, and Cajuns to act in concert, music added to their overall capacity to determine their own fates. In varying degrees, people used music as a communicative forum for identifying each other as members of a collective body with shared interests, for working out the commitments and (some of) the disagreements of this collective body, and for opening various political spaces in which this collective actor could engage in political practices to advance shared interests and negotiate differences. In a context of difference and diversity, the challenges of collective action became even greater and more pressing.

Of course, simply enabling political action does not ensure that the action produces the desired results. Acting in concert may be effective in making democratic change in peoples' lives, but it may be limited by its social and political context. These limitations help us appreciate the value of music as an *alternative* communicative forum. In each example in this book, music played an important role for people who had relatively few options. In the Chilean case, it provided a communicative arena for democratic socialists who were locked out of the major means of communication and, after the coup, lived under severe repression of all traditional forms of political interaction. In the American Indian and Cajun cases, music provided a communicative arena that was familiar and accessible and that functioned as an alternative to dominant and partly alien political arenas. Attempts to increase the political capacity of marginalized populations too often rely on eliminating the differences between marginalized and dominant populations. We saw this in both the American Indian and Cajun cases, when attempts by dominant policymakers to force assimilation broke up traditional ways of life and forced public education to follow an Anglo-European model. These tactics often require disconnection from the traditions and histories that provide the foundation for political subjectivity built on familiar ways of understanding the world and acting in it.[1] Building contemporary political subjectivity on a base of dynamic cultural practices avoids this problem of disconnection, and political action can emerge from a position of relative strength attached to familiar and proven ways of understanding and controlling the world. Relatively marginalized people are able to act politically on their own terms in ways that they define as appropriate.

Is this strategy effective in a larger context of political relations, including distant, dominant policymakers and other political actors and institutions? In each example I have discussed, music and related practices supported at least limited political success. In Chile, musicians helped form a collective actor on the political left that briefly won control of the presidency. After the coup they spread the word worldwide of Pinochet's abuses, encouraging international condemnation and helping Chileans maintain and recover the possibility of a democratic political system. In the Cajun case, it is entirely possible that Cajuns would not exist today as a distinctive people if it were not for music. The Cajun revival was initiated and sustained primarily by musicians, and the cultural and economic vitality of contemporary Cajuns depends significantly on their work. Although such a strong claim cannot be made for powwow music, it, too, has played an important role in helping Indian people survive in Minnesota and western Wisconsin and, more recently, begin taking steps to overcome social and political problems. Given the realities of power, American Indians and Cajuns must compromise, adapt, and accommodate. For both groups, music provided a vehicle for adaptation and accommodation while it helped them survive as a distinctive people.

There is much to learn from popular culture about contemporary issues in democratic theory such as self-determination, democratic participation, and the revitalization of communal and public life. Many people use popular culture to engage in practices that have democratic, political significance, and these practices merit more attention from political theorists than they have drawn thus far. One of my inescapable conclusions is that universal statements about the politics of music are difficult to make. Whether or not music plays a democratic role depends on many factors, including the degree to which it is tied to average peoples' daily lives, who controls it in whose interests, and the specific nature of power relations. Music is a communicative arena in which various political actors can pursue multiple, often contradictory, agendas in which there are no guarantees of a positive democratic outcome. It is one political terrain, among many.

Notes

Introduction

1. I observed and recorded each vignette during field research.
2. Although political theorists and political scientists have generally shunned the terrain of popular culture, there are some exceptions. Plato (1974, 90) may have been the first Western political philosopher to take seriously the political effects of music. He argued that "one should be cautious in adopting a new kind of . . . music, for this endangers the whole system." Centuries later, Luther (1965, 322) extolled the communicative capacity of music, saying that "next to the Word of God, music deserves the highest praise." Yet neither Plato nor Luther followed up on these observations with extensive treatments of the political significance of music. More recent exceptions include John Dewey (1925, 1934) and Antonio Gramsci (1971, 1985), both of whom wrote extensively on the potential political significance of art and popular culture. It will be evident throughout this book that I owe substantial intellectual debts to both thinkers.

Chapter 1 Popular Music and Community

1. See John Dewey (1916, 4), Robert Booth Fowler (1991, 3), and Chantal Mouffe (1991, 75) for three scholars of community who note that community entails commonality. See, especially, Fowler (1991, 3) on the contested nature of the concept of community.
2. Fowler identifies six roughly hewn "directions in contemporary thinking about community" that he calls participatory, republican, roots, globalist, religious, and existential, while freely acknowledging that "they do not begin to encompass the multitude of current explorations on the subject" of community (1991, 39). My characterization of a democratic political community fits most obviously into Fowler's populist face of participatory community (1991, 49–51), which involves "informal, grass roots, popular movements" among "concerned, active citizens" who are "informed by a 'broader vision of the common good'" and "empowered" to take "popular action."
3. Although it is difficult to ignore diversity today, not everyone agrees on the appropriate response to it. While some celebrate diversity and the multicultural commitments that they attach to it, others lament its disuniting consequences. For examples of the latter, see Arthur Schlesinger (1991) and Todd Gitlin (1995). Some critics charge that community is inconsistent with diversity, and their objection can be summarized as a question: is the "common" in community incompatible with multiple differences? See, for example, H. N. Hirsch

(1986) and Iris Young (1990) for liberal and postmodern critics of community, respectively. See also Fowler's (1991, 52–57) summary and discussion of some theorists' concerns that community is potentially hostile to freedom and diversity.

4. Other justifications include community as a tonic for moral drift and psychological alienation in an individualistic world, community as the social environment that best nurtures individual growth and development, and community as the basis for social order and stability. Ray Pratt (1990) exemplifies the first justification of community on psychological grounds, despite his generally political approach to understanding popular music. Pratt identifies an "unexpressed deeper and utopian longing" for community (7), calls community "a response to human alienation and longings" (24), and views communities derived from and around popular music as responses to these emotional and psychological needs. See, for example, John Winthrop, "A Modell of Christian Charity" (1630), for an eloquent defense of a Christian community that nurtures individual growth and development and forms the basis for social order and stability. See also John Dewey (1916, 1927, 1935, 1939), for whom community represented both an ideal social environment for individual growth and development and a social basis for collective political action.

5. See, especially, Chantal Mouffe (1991) on this point.

6. See, especially, Dewey (1930, 1935, 1939) for examples of his later discussions of effective freedom.

7. See Mouffe (1991), who emphasizes this first component of political identity. She discusses political identity in terms of "identification" with the democratic principles of "freedom and equality for all" (75). Dewey emphasized both components of political identity. In addition to recognizing the importance of a shared commitment to central democratic values and principles, he emphasized necessary skills and dispositions of individual citizens, as illustrated by his extensive work in civic education. See, for example, Dewey (1916, 1927, 1939).

8. See Rodolfo Alvarez et al. (1991, 4). By contemporary communitarians, I refer to the disparate group of signatories to "The Responsive Communitarian Platform: Rights and Responsibilities" (Alvarez et al. 1991). For discussions by and about contemporary communitarians, see, for example, Shlomo Avineri and Avner de-Shalit (1992), Daniel Bell (1993), and John Chapman and Ian Shapiro (1993).

9. See Hirsch (1986, 433–34) and Young (1990, 305) as examples of critics who object to community in part because, they argue, it requires face-to-face relationships. For an example of a theorist who defends community yet agrees with Hirsch and Young that it requires face-to-face relationships, see Boyte (1991b, 22), who asserts that "community politics is characterized by a 'Small Is Beautiful' view."

10. Other scholars have empirically tied popular music to community in useful and convincing ways. See, especially, John Miller Chernoff (1979) and Helen Kivnick (1990). See also Molefi Kete Asante and Kariamu Welsh Asante (1990), John Blacking (1973), Steven Feld (1982), Simon Frith (1989), LeRoi Jones (1963), Barbara Krader (1987), Peter Manuel (1989), Ray Pratt (1990), and Christopher Small (1987) for other examples of research that connects music to identity or community. While this literature establishes connections between music and identity or community, the connections are generally made apolitically and in ways that understate or ignore the consequences of diversity. In particular, these researchers have generally overlooked the role of mu-

sic in expressing, reinforcing, and negotiating differences and disagreements among members of a community.

11. Dewey recognized this quality of music, arguing that "sound agitates directly" and has the "power of direct emotional expression" (1934, 237–38). According to him, "the sounds emitted by musical instruments stir the atmosphere or the ground. They do not have to meet the opposition that is found in reshaping external material" (1934, 158). See also Raymond Williams (1961, 66–99), who argued that "rhythm is a way of transmitting a description of experience, in such a way that the experience is re-created in the person receiving it, not merely as an 'abstraction' or an emotion but as a physical effect on the organism—on the blood, on the breathing, on the physical patterns of the brain. . . . it is more than a metaphor; it is a physical experience as real as any other."

12. See, for example, Theodor W. Adorno (1932, 1948, 1962) and Susan McClary (1991). Adorno argued that "no matter where music is heard today, it sketches in the clearest possible lines the contradictions and flaws which cut through present-day society" (1932, 128). Although he exaggerated the clarity of musical meaning, he nevertheless recognized that music reflects its social environment and lends insight into it.

13. The appropriation of music can take decidedly perverse turns. Ray Pratt (1990, 5), for example, recounts a story of Margaret Thatcher's leading a crowd of conservative youth in a new conservative version of John Lennon's "Imagine." For a discussion of the politics of music reception, see especially Richard Leppert and Susan McClary (1987) and Simon Frith (1984).

14. For a discussion of these themes, see Jon Michael Spencer (1991). See also John Leland (1992), who quotes a *Billboard* article opining that "[t]he chicken-thieving, razor-toting 'coon' of the 1890s is the drug-dealing, Uzi-toting 'nigga' of today. . . . [The white] audience will eventually feel justified in all manner of acts of racism, predicated on Zip Coon stereotypes sold with the enthusiastic support of the entertainment industry."

15. This argument parallels the one for anthropology as cultural critique. Some anthropologists view their work as a tool for making critical comparisons among different ways of life. Through the ethnographic practices of description and interpretation, members of different "interpretive communities" (Fish 1980) engage in self-reflection and self-criticism while potentially reconstructing the boundaries of community in order to make them more inclusive, more open to change, more receptive to difference and diversity. Studying other cultures arms us to reflect critically on our own culture, which is made more transparent through the contrast to others. Toleration, respect for differences, and modesty in asserting universal claims are several of the values and commitments associated with the practice of anthropology as cultural critique. See, especially, George E. Marcus and Michael M. J. Fischer (1986) for a discussion of anthropology as cultural critique.

16. Several contemporary researchers have made a similar argument. Christopher Small (1987), Lewis A. Erenberg (1989), and David Bastien and Todd Hostager (1987) all argue that a musical tradition embodies values and assumptions about humans and human relationships and thus models a particular society. These values and assumptions are challenged and sometimes changed as musicians interact with each other and with musicians working in other traditions.

Chapter 2 *Popular Music, Political Action, and Power*

1. The three kinds of political action that I tie to musical practices are partially adapted from Harry Boyte (1991a), who uses the categories of deliberative, pragmatic, and insurgent (or protest). I call the third category confrontational to distance myself from some of the problems that Boyte identifies with the insurgent category, especially a view of citizenship that it may entail of permanent outsider, and to cluster a genre of political action that includes struggle, opposition, and resistance as well as protest.

2. See John Greenway (1977), Jerome L. Rodnitzky (1976) and Jeffery Mondak (1988) on protest music.

3. The work of Antonio Gramsci, an Italian Marxist writing in prison during the 1930s, has been widely used by researchers of cultural politics since its translation into English in 1971. See especially his *Prison Notebooks* (1971). In attempting to make sense of the apparent quiescence of the working class in Italy and internationally, an anomaly in Marxist theory, Gramsci turned to culture as an explanatory variable. He argued that dominant elites maintain control in part through ideological manipulation and control insinuated throughout culture. Because of the penetration into culture of bourgeois domination in the form of beliefs and ideologies of everyday life, workers believe in the legitimacy of the system that oppresses them. Under circumstances of bourgeois political, economic, and ideological domination—or hegemony—Gramsci advocated a "war of position" in venues of everyday life, including popular music, to challenge dominant elites. Many scholars have used this framework to interpret cultural politics. See, for example, Tim Patterson's (1975) interpretation of country-and-western music and Manuel Peña's (1985) interpretation of Texas-Mexican conjunto music for explicit applications of Gramsci to popular music. See also George Lewis's (1991) interpretation of Hawaiian popular music, which is less explicitly indebted to Gramsci but couched in similar terms. For other examples of literature, much of it indebted to Gramsci, that emphasizes the resistant and oppositional nature of music, see Horace Campbell (1987), Dick Hebdige (1987), and Patrick Hylton (1975) on calypso and reggae; Charles Keil (1979) on African TIV music; Peter Manuel (1989) on Andalusian gypsy music; Ray Pratt (1990) on several forms of popular music; Tricia Rose (1994) on rap; and Kilza Setti (1988) on Brazilian Caicara music.

4. See Renato Rosaldo's (1988) discussion of border zones, which challenges the traditional anthropological view of a culture as an "autonomous internally coherent universe" (87). According to Rosaldo, cultures are less self-contained and homogeneous now than ever before. Rather, our world is "marked by borrowing and lending across porous cultural boundaries," and social space is "crisscrossed by border zones, pockets, and eruptions of all kinds" (1988, 87). See also Gloria Anzaldúa (1987).

5. This can be seen more clearly by briefly examining the roots of the concept of dialogism. Rose adapted the concept from George Lipsitz (1990, 99–132), who uses it in the context of rock and roll to indicate a "historical conversation" in which contemporary popular music builds upon "the recovery and re-accentuation of previous works" (99). Rock and roll, Lipsitz argues, is "a dialogic space, an arena where memories of the past serve to critique and change the present" (100). In Lipsitz's work, then, dialogism is less about contemporary musicians discussing and debating politically among themselves than about contemporary musicians borrowing from the past to express themselves in the

present. Although Rose politicizes the concept more than Lipsitz does, she also appears to use it in nonpolitical ways akin to Lipsitz's "historical conversation."

6. This pragmatic form of acting in concert builds upon the visions of public life articulated by John Dewey (1927) and, more recently, Harry Boyte (1989, 1992). Both emphasize that "the aim of politics is common action on significant public problems," which entails "the ability to work pragmatically with a variety of others" (Boyte 1992, 7). Both emphasize collaborative and cooperative forms of problem solving and distance themselves from confrontational forms of political action. Both emphasize the importance of civic education and widespread and responsible participation in public life by average citizens. Both use the concept of community extensively. However, while Dewey generally failed to theorize the specific character of community-based problem solving—its sites, its institutional and organizational bases—Boyte has developed a robust and detailed picture of the actual work of citizen politics that emphasizes engaged citizen action on shared concerns and issues in a variety of arenas.

7. See, for example, Thomas Wartenberg (1990) for both a summary of this basic distinction and a challenge to it. Wartenberg challenges the notion that all forms of "power over" are necessarily about domination. He distinguishes between domination and what he calls "transformative power," which involves an unequal exercise of power aimed at empowering someone. His paradigmatic example is the transformative power exercised by a parent over a child.

8. For example, in his study of heavy metal music, Rob Walser (1993) argues that the "loudness and intensity of heavy metal music visibly empower fans, whose shouting and headbanging testify to the circulation of energy at concerts. Metal energizes the body" (2), which translates into the listener's perception of increased power. Heavy metal musicians produce these psychological and affective responses through power chords, heavy amplification, vocal and instrumental distortion, electronic sustain, and other conventions. In addition to the power chords they produce and sustain electronically, heavy metal singers produce "aural distortion through excessive power . . . as the capacities of the vocal chords are exceeded," which "functions as a sign of extreme power and intense expression by overflowing its channels and materializing the exceptional effort that produces it" (42). Ray Pratt (1990) makes a similar argument, writing that "moments of emotional release, cathartic episodes in concerts in which one 'gets outside oneself' in joy, carry both prefigurative and affectively empowering implications. . . . By being empowered one is energized rather than depressed; one might sense the possibility of enormous and positive changes, rather than being overwhelmed by the immensity of what only apparently cannot be accomplished" (37–39). See also Tricia Rose (1994, 138), who argues that the rhythmic pulse of rap music "energizes" and "empowers" listeners; and Lawrence Grossberg, "Another Boring Day in Paradise: Rock and Roll and the Empowerment of Everyday Life" (1984).

9. See, for example, Bernice Johnson Reagon, "The Power of Communal Song" (1985). A program with the same title aired over National Public Radio on February 6, 1994, and described the role of songs such as "We Shall Overcome" in helping civil rights workers maintain courage and resolve.

10. For a summary and application of the three faces of power, see John Gaventa (1980). See Peter Digeser (1992) for a discussion of a fourth face of power, derived primarily from the work of Michel Foucault, that is "productive of subjects, accompanied by resistance, twined with knowledge, . . . insidious,

totalizing, individuating, and disciplinary." It is "power operating in structures of thinking and behavior" that determine human identity (977).

11. Mark Fenster (1990) describes such an attempt by country music recording executives to control the music of Buck Owens. According to Fenster, this "struggle for discursive control" between Owens and other members of the country music industry involved attempts to control the production, meaning, and use of Owens's music.

12. This connection between music and a third face of power is best exemplified by the theorists who use a Gramscian-Marxist framework for analysis. Gramsci believed that cultural forms such as music play a role in either legitimizing current forms of control and domination or undermining them in a counter-hegemonic struggle. For him, power includes various forms of ideological control and means of socialization that enable a current class in power to perpetuate prevailing beliefs and assumptions and contribute to a situation in which the ideological supports for domination come to be internalized as common sense. The role of musicians, like other cultural workers, thus becomes either one of perpetuating these legitimizing ideologies, beliefs, and assumptions or challenging them. Although this Gramscian framework captures an important connection between music and the third face of power, theorists using the framework too often conceive of power in either-or terms. One group's gain in power is another's loss: either a group is in power (hegemonic) or out of power (counter-hegemonic). There is little room for shared power or the cooperative creation of new forms of power.

13. Similarly, Michael Cary (1990) argues that blues music "give[s] voice to powerlessness. Blues lyrics are filled with the pain which comes from an inability to control the important events of one's life." Blues music, he argues, reflects the experiences of powerlessness both in lyrical themes of travel and escape and in its repetitive musical structure, which "signifies both confined possibilities . . . and conscious, honest recognition of this situation" (41–44). Although blues music reflects relative powerlessness, Cary argues that it also provides a counteractive ideology for its listeners. In other words, he does not reduce blues music merely to being a passive reflector of other power relations, as does Adorno. See also Susan McClary (1991), who interprets music in terms of what it reveals about relations of power between genders.

14. Although this connection between power and popular music has been noted by other researchers, the connection remains largely implicit in their work. For example, Hylton (1975, 23, 24) argues that at one time calypso played the role of "people's political mouthpiece" and "poor man's newspaper." Campbell (1987) argues that African people "developed musical forms which were means of both communication and inspiration" in resistance to slavery (125). Paul Gilroy (1987) argues that music functions within the culture of the black diaspora as an alternative public sphere.

Chapter 3 **El pueblo, unido, jamás será vencido**

1. "El pueblo, unido, jamás será vencido" [the people, united, will never be defeated] (1973) is one of the most famous songs by the Chilean group Quilapayún. Testifying to the revolutionary spirit in Chile of the 1960s and early 1970s, the song eventually became a rallying cry for progressive political movements throughout the world. It summarizes the efforts of Chilean musicians during 1960–73 to organize for democratic transformation.

I conducted field research for this chapter in Santiago, Chile, during the summer of 1989 and the spring of 1991. All translations are mine, with assistance from Alicia del Campo.

2. Election returns illustrate this polarization. With the exception of the Christian Democrats during the 1960s, no single party received more than 30 percent of the popular vote in congressional or municipal elections between 1925 and 1973. Between 1937 and 1973, the vote for the left averaged 21.5 percent (this figure is higher—25.7 percent—if account is taken of the three years in which Communists were banned from participation), and the vote for parties on the right averaged 30.1 percent.

3. See, especially, J. Samuel Valenzuela and Arturo Valenzuela (1985) and Brian Loveman (1997) for modern political histories of Chile. See Eduardo Carrasco (1982, 1988) and Luis Cifuentes (1989) for discussions of Chilean culture that emphasize its ruptures and discontinuities.

4. See, especially, Carrasco (1982) and Fernando Reyes Matta (1988) for overviews of the "new song" movement in Latin America.

5. The two most popular folk singers in Chilean history were Violeta Parra and Victor Jara. Parra is often called the mother of nueva canción chilena. Jara's music filled approximately sixty record releases despite the fact that he began his career in theater, not music, and was executed by the Pinochet junta at the age of thirty-eight. To appreciate his stature as an artist and a beloved cultural figure, we might think of him as a composite of John Lennon, Bob Dylan, and Woody Guthrie.

6. Carrasco (1988, 68, 75). One of the most important nueva canción groups of this period was Quilapayún, formed in 1965 by university students in Santiago. Members of the group saw their task as addressing the "absence of authenticity" in Chilean culture, which was increasingly dominated by foreign influences, especially European, Anglo, and North American. They set out to recover an authentic Chilean identity, to answer the question of who they were as Chileans, to discover their roots and origins, and to answer the question of Chilean cultural inconsistency. This meant that they needed to reconcile the European with the Latin American, the Spanish with the Indian, the African with the North American (Carrasco 1988, 21–22).

7. Pérez Zujović was assassinated soon after the appearance of Jara's song. No one was ever identified or charged with the crime, but Jara was blamed by many on the political right, who claimed that his song had fanned the hatred behind the assassination.

8. For example, the premier edition of its *Revista de Folklore* (1970) featured prominent advertisements by unions such as La Federación Eléctrica [the electrical federation] and La Confederación Nacionál de Trabajadores del Cobre [the national confederation of copper workers].

9. See also, for example, Victor Jara's "Angelita Huenumán" (1965) in which he sang about the simple but creative and dignified life of a woman from the marginalized rural areas whom he met on one of his many tours of the Chilean countryside.

10. Huenchullán was the name of a Mapuche, or Araucanian, Indian chief. The Mapuche are the primary indigenous people of Chile. They were dubbed Araucanians by the Spanish but prefer their own name. Other examples of songs that either called attention to the marginalized status of the Mapuche or described their everyday lives are Parra's "El guillatún," a description of a Mapuche

harvest and religious ceremony, and Patricio Manns's "La Araucana," in which he also exhorted the Mapuche people to stand up.

11. Other examples include Violeta Parra's "Al centro de la injusticia" [at the heart of injustice], which criticized a social system in which "the miner produces much wealth, but for the pocket of the foreigner," and "Y arriba quemando el sol" [and the sun is burning above], which decried the oppressive living conditions of miners living in northern Chile.

12. Also in this vein, in the late 1960s Inti-Illimani recorded Kuben Lenna's "Simón Bolívar," a tribute to Simon Bolivar, and Lenna's "La segunda independencia" [the second independence], which called for Latin American unity in opposition to the imperialists from the north.

13. *Comandante* and *compañero* are references to Fidel Castro. Quilapayún also recorded a tribute to Guevara, "Canción fúnebre para el Che Guevara" [funeral song for Che Guevara] (1968). Several songs were recorded during this period attacking the U.S. policy on Vietnam. Examples include Quilapayún's "Por Vietnam" [for Vietnam] (1968) and Victor Jara's "El derecho de vivir en paz" [the right to live in peace] (1971).

14. Most of the histories of, and commentaries on, the period have been written with an eye toward class rather than ethnicity or race (or gender), so little evidence regarding indigenous populations can be found in history books. Histories of Chilean nueva canción by Carrasco (1982, 1988) and Cifuentes (1989) emphasize its mass following, drawn both from lower and middle classes.

15. Because Allende had fallen short of an absolute electoral majority, the Chilean congress, following constitutional procedure, had to elect the winner from the two leading candidates. Despite pressure from the United States, the congress followed tradition and elected Allende, the frontrunner. His election marked the first time that a coalition dominated by Marxist parties took control of the Chilean executive.

16. The U.S. Senate Select Committee, headed by Senator Frank Church of Idaho, discovered that the CIA had funneled more than $8 million into the destabilization campaign against Allende between 1969 and 1973 for covert activities ranging from "simple propaganda manipulation of the press to large-scale support for Chilean political parties, from public opinion polls to direct attempts to foment a military coup" (Chavkin 1989, 40). Some of this money went directly to Chilean oppositional forces such as the conservative daily newspaper *El Mercurio;* some was funneled through U.S. corporations active in Chile such as International Telephone and Telegraph Corporation (ITT). Economic sabotage included a U.S.–instituted embargo on Chile's copper exports and on spare parts, a massive truckers' strike funded in part with CIA dollars, and artificial shortages of consumer goods such as toilet paper. (Jorge Alessandri, Allende's opponent in the 1969 presidential election, owned the toilet paper factory.) See, especially, Chavkin's (1989, 39–80) account of the turbulent Allende years.

17. See Cifuentes's (1989, 76–98) account of Inti-Illimani's role in the Allende presidency and Carrasco's (1988, 221–42) account of Quilapayún's role.

18. The popular expression "ni chicha ni limoná" could more loosely be translated as "neither one thing nor another."

19. Valenzuela and Valenzuela (1985, 235–36) make a similar interpretation, citing as the primary reason for the coup the "inability and unwillingness of moderate forces on both sides of the political dividing line to forge center agreements on programs and policies as well as on regime-saving compromises."

20. Unfortunately, exact sales figures on recordings are unavailable, having been destroyed after the coup. Some evidence is available anecdotally. For example, in his history of Quilapayún, Carrasco notes that their long-play "Por Vietnam," released in 1968, sold out immediately and was subsequently reissued several times in an attempt to keep up with demand. He also notes that the song "Arriba en la cordillera" [up in the mountains] by Patricio Manns, released during the same period, "broke all the records for popularity on the country's radio stations" that agreed to play it (1988, 132, 151).

Chapter 4   Vamos a vivir

1. "Vamos a vivir" [we are going to live] was recorded by the group Nepalé in the early 1980s. Literally, the song title means that Chileans will survive the physical brutality of the dictatorship; metaphorically, that democracy will survive.
2. The military seized Victor Jara on the day after the coup, tortured him, and several days later executed him. Quilapayún and Inti-Illimani were both on international tours at the time of the coup and remained abroad. (Violeta Parra had committed suicide in 1967.) Exiled nueva canción musicians used their music in the subsequent fifteen years to maintain a community of exiles and generate worldwide opposition to Pinochet.
3. For more detailed accounts of this period, see José Joaquín Brunner, Alicia Barrios, and Carlos Catalán (1989, 43–60); Samuel Chavkin (1989); Ricardo García (1987); and Luis Mella, Carlos Catalán, Anny Rivera, and Rodrigo Torres (1980, 3–8).
4. See, especially, Alvaro Godoy's (1981, 6–7) discussion of the many challenges facing musicians after the military coup.
5. Given the need to mute their political messages, the musicians sang instead about traditional folklore (Pedro Yáñez); pain and the desire for justice (Nano Acevedo); Eastern mystical harmony and salvation (Los Blops); the lives of Andean Indians (Illapu); the communal values of the Indio (Osvaldo Torres); the everyday lives of the people of Chiloe, an island off the southern coast of Chile (Chamal); materialism and a shallow life (Cantierra); the pitfalls of passivity (Santiago del Nuevo Extremo); human rights without specific reference to Chile (Ortiga and Aquelarre); and a frustrated future, a realistic hope, living according to certain ideals, and the social contradictions of poverty and misery (Eduardo Peralta). Many of these musicians and groups attempted to counter the new market-inspired values of consumerism, individualism, and competition and to combine themes of justice and liberty (expressed in general terms without reference to Chile) with themes of personal dilemma, love, and Christianity.
6. Other examples included Violeta Parra's prophetic "La carta" [the letter], describing the arrest of her brother for supporting a work stoppage and bemoaning the lack of justice in her homeland, where hungry people ask for bread but receive military bullets instead. She concluded:
   Luckily I have a guitar
   and also I have my voice.
   Also I have seven brothers
   besides the one in chains.
   All of them are revolutionaries,
   thanks to God. Yes!
   Another of Parra's songs that was popular after the coup, covered prominently

by canto nuevo musician Isabel Aldunate, was "Qué dirá el Santo Padre" [I wonder what the Holy Father is saying?]:

> Look how they speak to us of liberty
> when in reality they deprive us of it.
> Look how they proclaim tranquility
> while the authorities torment us. . . .
> Look how they speak to us of paradise
> while raining sorrow on us like hail.

7. According to Nano Acevedo, director of Peña Doña Javiera, his audience members showed a great "eagerness to remember" and to listen to sounds and words evoking an epoch (Rivera 1980, 30–31).

8. These figures represent the results of a joint survey conducted in 1987 by the Facultad Latinoamericana de Ciencias Sociales (FLACSO) and the Centro de Endagación y Expresión Cultural y Artística (CENECA). Between 1970 and 1981, the importation of prerecorded cassettes increased by 3,523 percent from $31,900 in value to $2,761,000. During the same period, the importation of blank tapes increased by 4,060 percent from $244,000 in value to $5,920,000. Between 1970 and 1981 the importation of cassette recorders increased by 1,945 percent from $271,600 in value to $5,554,000. Between 1977 and 1981, the importation of cassette players increased by 457 percent from $348,200 in value to $1,983,000. Figures are not available for 1970–76 on the importation of cassette players. See Rivera (1984, 39–41), who gathered her data from the Import Register of the Central Bank of Chile.

9. After the coup García attempted to return to work as a disc jockey but the doors were closed. The logo for Alerce shows one fallen alerce tree, symbolizing the dispersion of nueva canción, and one standing, symbolizing the rebirth of popular song in canto nuevo.

10. See Rivera (1980). Ninety-five percent of peña goers responded in a survey that they listened regularly to recorded Chilean music (Rivera 1980, 17), indicating a taste for indigenous popular music that accompanied and perhaps replaced a taste for the imported music that was more readily available in mainstream media. Fifty-three percent said that they listened regularly to nueva canción musicians (Rivera 1980, 19), showing that the music of the exiles was widely available and familiar inside Chile despite official policies discouraging its circulation.

11. See Chavkin (1989, 237–78).

12. Alvaro Godoy, essayist and editor of the popular cultural magazines *La Bicicleta* and *La Cigarra*, estimated in 1981 that Chilean youth listened to imported rock music 90 percent of the time and to Chilean rock music most of the remaining time (Godoy 1981, 9).

13. Although peñas were important public and political spaces during the 1970s and early 1980s, by the mid- to late 1980s they were less important, given the widespread circulation of cassette recordings and the growing availability of other public spaces.

14. Canto nuevo is still sometimes referred to as *whizquierda*, a word combining *whiskey* (Chileans use the same word that Anglos do) and *izquierda*, the Spanish word for "left." Because whiskey is imported and expensive in Chile, and therefore consumed mostly by the upper and upper middle classes, whizquierda satirizes canto nuevo's upper-class radicalism.

15. The term *canto poblacional* is from Rivera (1980). See also Rivera and Torres (1981) and Rivera (1983) for discussions of canto poblacional.

16. Rivera and Torres (1981, 34–35) estimate that "more than half" of the canto poblacional songs were original compositions. Their findings are consistent with my own experiences in 1989 and 1991. Most of the musicians that I met drew on a large repertoire of nueva canción and canto nuevo songs but also wrote many original compositions in which they expressed sentiments on topics ranging from their economic and familial situations to general condemnations of political life in Chile.

17. The "mourning women . . . dressed in black" are the mothers of Chileans who have been detained or who have disappeared.

18. Throughout Santiago, bus drivers typically allow vendors and performers to board their bus without paying. These vendors and performers remain on a bus only long enough to work the crowd and then disembark to board the next bus that comes along.

19. I observed and recorded each of these scenes, and many others like them, during June and July 1989.

20. Poets, clowns, actors, writers, and orators also appeared in the streets of Santiago, attempting, like musicians, to open public spaces to express political messages of opposition to Pinochet and affirm democratic alternatives—and, not incidentally, earn some extra pesos. Political expression in the streets sometimes took comical forms. For example, in 1985 opponents of Pinochet dropped several hundred balls from the tall buildings facing Paseo Ahumado, a crowded pedestrian mall in downtown Santiago, each with a picture of Pinochet on it. Pedestrians enjoyed kicking the balls around, as police scurried to retrieve them. See Chavkin (1989, 277–78) for a brief description of this process of politicization during the early and mid-1980s.

21. Some of these musicians and groups attained international recognition and popularity. Inti-Illimani found itself at one point competing in Italy with the rock group Pink Floyd for top position on the sales charts (Cifuentes 1989, 233).

22. The 1988 plebescite, in which Chileans voted yes or no to eight more years of Pinochet, illustrated how divided Chilean society remained. Although outsiders often assume that a large majority of Chileans opposed the 1973 coup and favored a return to democratic government, many Chileans celebrated when Pinochet seized power, a majority voted for him in a 1980 referendum giving him eight more years as president, and 43 percent faithfully supported him in 1988. Remarkably, even after fifteen years of state-sponsored terrorism, nearly half of the Chilean voting population still preferred the dictatorship to a return to democracy.

Chapter 5 **Laissez les bon temps roulez**

1. *Laissez les bon temps roulez* translates as "let the good times roll" and is often considered the rallying cry for both Cajun and zydeco music.

2. Other observers also emphasize the degree to which Cajun music is intertwined with the history and culture of its people. For example, according to John Broven (1983, 8), Cajun music is the "chief artistic expression of the Cajun culture," expressing both the spirit and history of the people. Ann A. Savoy (1984, xi) argues that "describing Cajun music would be like summarizing . . . the evolution of a people."

3. For excellent histories of Acadian settlement, dispersal, resettlement, and development in Louisiana, see Carl A. Brasseaux (1987, 1991, 1992).

4. See, for example, Brasseaux (1987, 147) and Marjorie R. Esman (1985, 104).

5. See Barry Jean Ancelet (1989) and Robert Gilmore and Jeanne Gilmore (1970, 1977) for collections of songs whose lyrics reflect Cajun history. They cite songs from collections recorded in twentieth-century southwest Louisiana, some originating in France, others in Nova Scotia.

6. See, especially, Brasseaux (1992) for a history of Cajuns' waning economic fortunes.

7. This traditional song was recorded by Beausoleil in 1977 (*Beausoleil* [Swallow Records]).

8. For extended discussions of the development of Cajun music, see, especially, Ancelet (1984, 1989), Savoy (1984), and Broven (1983).

9. See Brasseaux (1992, 100) for a brief discussion of negative portrayals of Cajuns in national media. According to him, they were portrayed as "debased and tainted" by slavery; their relatively modest material ambitions made them "lazy and unambitious" as well as "backward"; their Catholicism made them "priest-dominated, intolerant of other faiths, and pawns in the Pope's perceived quest for world domination"; their strong extended family ties made them "dangerously inbred"; their lack of formal education made them "ignorant" or even "stupid"; and their refusal to assimilate made them "un-American."

10. See, for example, Esman (1985, 51,56). This is consistent with the findings of Harald Eidheim (1970), whose study of Lapps living in Norway also indicates that a common response to ethnic stigma is to avoid revealing the stigmatized traits in public or even avoiding public encounters in the first place.

11. The translation is by Ancelet (1992a).

12. See *Louisiana Cajun French Music Association: Laisse le bon temps rouler*, vol. 1, trans. Melissa Fiutak (CFMA Records 02 [Acadia Music]). See also Zachary Richard's "Ma Louisiane" (on Mardi Gras, RZ 1005) in which he reminds his listeners of their collective history and asserts his pride in his Cajun identity:

    Me, I am proud to be Cajun. . . .
    Thank God for Louisiana.

    See also the Balfa Brothers' 1975 recording of "Je suis content d'être un Cajun" [I'm happy to be a Cajun] (Rounder, 6007).

13. Soileau's labels include Jin, Swallow, and Maison de Soul. Miller's labels include Fais Do Do and Feature.

14. The translation is by Ancelet (1992a).

15. For a history of this period of the Cajun revival, including a discussion of the first Tribute to Cajun Music, see especially Ancelet (1992a).

16. Traditional, as translated by Savoy (1984, 84).

17. One example of this effort to draw connections through music was the Balfa Brothers' recording in Cajun style of the French children's folk tune "J'ai vu le loup, le renard et la belette" [I saw the wolf, the fox, and the weasel], which they had learned while touring France in 1975. This recording introduced something from France directly into contemporary life in southwest Louisiana and affirmed cultural and kinship ties with the French people. One example of a festival designed to highlight cultural connections was the 1982 Festival de Musique Acadienne, which presented a slate of performers from French-speaking communities throughout North America, including some from French Canada and the Michoff Indian tribe of North Dakota.

18. The other nominees were black Creoles, including Clifton Chenier, Stanley "Buckwheat Zydeco" Dural, and Rockin' Sidney (Sidney Simien). Rockin' Sidney ultimately won with his "Don't Mess With My Toot-Toot."

19. Examples include the National Council for the Traditional Arts of the National

Endowment for the Arts; the Louisiana Folklife Program of the Louisiana Department of Culture, Recreation, and Tourism; the Center for Louisiana Studies at the University of Southwestern Louisiana; and the Louisiana State Arts Council. All provided funding for Octa Clark and Hector Duhon's *Dixie Rambler,* a long-play recording released in 1982 (Rounder 6011). The city of Lafayette partially supports two Cajun heritage theme parks, Vermillionville and Acadiana; and the state legislature recently designated southwest Louisiana as "Acadiana" to help promote tourism.

20. The Festival de Musique Acadienne replaced the annual Tribute to Cajun Music. Downtown Alive! takes place in downtown Lafayette each Friday after work in an attempt to maintain the vitality of the city by encouraging people to stay there and patronize its bars, clubs, and restaurants. An intersection is blocked off for live music and dancing. Downtown Alive! is sometimes complemented by Kids Alive!, with performers such as the Children's Cajun Band.

21. A partial list of pressures includes mainstream media forms and influences, dwindling opportunities for the use of the French language, increasing social mobility, and remnants of ethnic stigma. Part of the value of Cajun music is that it provides at least one substantial bulwark against these assimilating influences.

22. For example, the 1993 Festival de Musique Acadienne was opened by Kristy Guillory and Réveille, featuring three Lafayette High School students, ages fourteen through seventeen. Children regularly dance in public events such as Le Cajun music awards and festivals sponsored by the Cajun French Music Association.

23. For a list of Cajun music and dance venues, see Macon Fry and Julie Posner (1992, 77–78).

24. Prominent women include Kristy Guillory, Sheryl Cormier, Becky Richard, Grosby Vidrine, Ann Savoy, Sharon Doucet, and Nelda and Christine Balfa. Examples of award winners include Becky Richard, who won a Le Cajun (CFMA award) in 1992, and Sheryl Cormier, the 1989 winner of Acadian Village's "le musicien de bal."

Chapter 6   **Stirring Up the Roux**

1. I was that lone "tourist." October is off-peak season for tourists in Louisiana.

2. For example, in October and November 1993 in Lafayette, radio station KRVS, 88.7 FM, played Cajun music Monday through Friday from 5:00 A.M. to 7:00 A.M. and on Sunday from 6:00 A.M. to 5:00 P.M.. In Eunice, considered by many to be the heart of Cajun country, station KUEN, 1490 AM, played Cajun music Monday through Friday from 5:00 A.M. to 6:30 A.M.; Saturday from 5:00 A.M. to 8:30 A.M,. 9:00 A.M. to 11:00 A.M. live from Carriers Lounge, and 6:00 P.M. to midnight; and Sundays from 5:30 A.M. to noon. In nearby Opelousas, station KSLO, 1230 AM, Cajun music aired from 5:00 A.M. to 7:00 A.M. Monday through Saturday, on Saturdays from 10:00 A.M. to noon, and on alternate Saturdays from 7:00 P.M. to 10:00 P.M. live from Church Point. These examples highlight stations that play Cajun music relatively frequently. Others play it even less often. On weekdays after about 7:00 A.M. the airwaves are dominated by country-and-western, rock, and pop. On weekends, Cajun music is easier to find on the radio, but it is still not as widely played as mainstream music. Barry Ancelet, acting as master of ceremonies for the fourth biennial *Times of Acadiana* Music Awards ceremony, held in September 1993, publicly chastised local radio

stations for not playing enough home-grown music (Huggs 1993, 11). But station owners are likely to have done their market research and would presumably argue that they are only responding to consumers' tastes.

3. Even in mainstay Cajun restaurants such as Louivere's in Lafayette, which advertises "a Cajun working man's lunch," the jukebox typically plays country-and-western throughout the lunch hours. At Carrier's Lounge in Eunice, which hosts a Saturday afternoon Cajun fais do-do, bar patrons on Friday and Saturday nights listen almost exclusively to country-and-western on the jukebox. The majority of the patrons who attended the famous Saturday morning radio broadcast that I attended in Fred's Lounge in Mamou were fifty years of age or older. A tour bus of senior citizens arrived to skew the sample, but the average age even before their arrival was over fifty (my estimate). At the "Rendez-vous" later at the Liberty Theater in Eunice, although there were several children and teens and perhaps one-fourth were young adults, the majority in the audience were senior citizens (observations recorded by author, October and November 1993).

4. I am grateful to Barry Ancelet for this information.

5. Balfa cites Bob Wills of Texas Playboys fame as one of his primary influences (Ancelet 1981, 79). The music of contemporary innovator Wayne Toups is described as "a sound infused with good, healthy doses of traditional Cajun a la Iry Lejeune, overlaid with upbeat jazz rhythms, country and a touch of rock" (Booth 1985, 42). The style of Beausoleil's Michael Doucet has been described as a blend of "vast historic knowledge with aggressive eclecticism and brilliant technique. Doucet has played rock, and he understands avante-garde jazz. Such wild influences are amply evident in his daring rhythmic/harmonic forays" (Sandmel 1984). Zachary Richard says that his music is "a holy trinity mix of Cajun, Zydeco, and New Orleans rhythm and blues cooked in a rock-n-roll pot" (Simon 1993, A13).

6. It is not only aficionados and tourists who demand "authenticity." Organizations such as the Smithsonian Institute, which sponsors the annual Smithsonian Festival of American Folklife, invites musicians who they believe will portray authentic surviving cultures. This often includes Cajun musicians.

7. Only one of the photographs in Gould's collection apparently includes both whites and blacks, and the setting is a public beach. The book reveals a near-absolute segregation of social space at musical events. My personal observations and interviews conducted in southern Louisiana in October and November 1993 confirmed this strict separation of whites and blacks according to Cajun and zydeco.

8. Different zydeco musicians incorporate different influences. The zydeco of Clifton Chenier and "Buckwheat Zydeco" Dural reflects a strong rhythm-and-blues influence, and the zydeco of Terrance Simien, while incorporating elements as diverse as reggae, is most obviously influenced by soul. "Rockin' Dopsie" Rubin, Sr., described his zydeco as a blend of French, blues, and jazz (Mills 1982, 25E). Jude Taylor of Jude Taylor and the Burning Flames Zydeco Band calls zydeco a mixture of French, blues, and up-tempo jazz (Dufilho 1989).

9. Among the most prominent contemporary women zydeco performers are Ann Goodly, known as the princess of zydeco; Theresa Leday of Pee Wee and the Zydeco Boll Weevils; Deborah Kennedy, who plays lead guitar for Zydeco Joe and the Laissez Les Bons Temps Rouler Band; and (Queen) Ida Guillory and her Bon Temps Band. Although Queen Ida is probably best known outside of

Louisiana and most associated with zydeco, her brand of zydeco is distinctively Californian and the one that is least inspired by African influences.

10. For example, in the April 20–25, 1993, Festival Internationale in downtown Lafayette, groups represented South Africa, Congo/Quebec, Haiti, Corsica, France, Cambodia, Madagascar, Guadeloupe, Martinique, French Guiana, Belgium, Senegal, the Canadian Maritimes, the former Soviet Union, Cuba, and the Dominican Republic as well as southwest Louisiana.

11. Watters's story on racial tension was published in Lafayette's *The Times of Acadiana* (September 29, 1993) and reprinted in *The Nation* (November 22, 1993).

12. The committee organizing the 1980 Festival de Musique Acadienne promoted the upcoming festival with a poster featuring Canray Fontenot, the black Creole fiddler. In a later year, the festival was dedicated to Amédée Ardoin, the black Creole musician considered by many to be the godfather of traditional Cajun accordion style, and the same festival focused on contributions by black Creoles to Cajun music.

13. The French title included with Ancelet's book is *Musiciens cadiens et créoles* [Cajun and Creole musicians].

14. In his book *South to Louisiana: The Music of the Cajun Bayous* (1983), John Broven describes zydeco as music sung by "black Cajuns" (1983, 101). Chris Strachwitz, owner of the California-based Arhoolie label, which helped bring the music of southwest Louisiana to a national and international audience, calls Amédée Ardoin "the first black Cajun recording artist." See liner notes to the 1991 cassette of the same title. In 1981, KEUN radio in Eunice began broadcasting an hour of zydeco on Saturday mornings, announcing that "zydeco, traditional black Cajun music, has been neglected by Southwest Louisiana radio stations for years" (Broven 1983, 116). The reference to Amédée Ardoin as a "black Cajun" especially grates on black Creoles, who revere him as a cultural godfather. It distorts the cultural record and implicitly condones what some black Creoles view as the theft of cultural property—for example, by Cajun musicians such as Iry LeJeune, who profited from Amédée's artistry. It is worth pointing out that "virtually no African-Americans in [southwest Louisiana], neither of English-speaking nor of French-speaking backgrounds, identify themselves as Cajuns" (Ancelet 1992c, 42).

15. *Zydeco: Cajun/Creole/Bayou Music* (GNP Crescendo 2101, 1976). This example is especially unfortunate because Queen Ida is a black Creole.

16. *Zydeco*, so the story goes, is the phonetic rendering of "haricots." The Creole French spoken by many black Creoles in southern Louisiana was until recently strictly an oral language; thus, spellings for various words needed to be invented. The term *zydeco* has been in circulation for a long time, but only in 1960 did ethnomusicologist Mack McCormick attempt to render it in writing. Occasionally the word is rendered as *zodico*. The Plaisance zydeco festival brochure announces that the word is pronounced "Zah-dee-ko."

17. Clarence Garlow's "Bon Ton Roula," recorded in the late 1940s, contained a direct reference to this meaning of zydeco as an event: "At the church bazaar or the baseball game, / At the French La La, it's all the same, / You want to have fun, now you got to go / Way out in the country to the Zydeco. / Well, let the Bon Ton Roula" (Broven 1983, 105).

18. See Barry Jean Ancelet (1992c, 42) and Takuna Maulana El Shabazz (1992, 45) for examples of these accusations. Making matters worse, in El Shabazz's view, black Creoles must help pay for their own colonization because tax money

is now routinely dedicated to the promotion of Cajun tourism. This, he says, "is taxation without representation, and misuse and abuse of public funds" (1992, 43). He accuses Kenny Bowen, mayor of Lafayette, of "represent[ing] and support[ing] a government that uses public funds to produce Niggers," or black people bereft of an African consciousness and denied an ability for self-determination.

19. Some zydeco musicians now take steps to ensure that their music is appropriately described and promoted as zydeco rather than Cajun. For example, "Buckwheat Zydeco" Dural inserted in his performing contract a clause forbidding the use of the term *Cajun* for promotional or descriptive purposes. Like El Shabazz, he denies any hostile intent toward Cajuns. According to Dural, "instead of one culture, what we have here is two. And both of them are good. We have two good things going" (Ancelet 1992a, xviii).

20. Examples include Herbert Wiltz's Saturday morning radio show on the University of Southwestern Louisiana campus radio, dominated by zydeco but also including black Creole French lessons, interviews with black Creole musicians and activists, and other discussions of black Creole culture; and Don Cravins's weekly zydeco television program (channel 15, 11:30 A.M. on Saturdays) and weekly zydeco radio program (KNEK 104.7 FM).

21. Two other organizations that occasionally promote zydeco are CREOLE, Inc. (Cultural Resourceful Educational Opportunities for Linguistic Enrichment) and *Creole Magazine*. CREOLE, Inc., was formed in 1988 to create an awareness of cultural differences in southwest Louisiana between black Creoles and Cajuns and to promote black Creole culture, especially its African elements. *Creole Magazine* covers many issues of concern to black Creoles in the region, including cultural expressions such as zydeco; promotes black Creole political, social, economic and cultural interests; offers Creole French lessons; and serves as an information vehicle for black Creoles in southwest Louisiana.

Chapter 7   Entering the Circle

1. The term *powwow* derives from a Narragansett Algonquian word *pauau*, initially meaning a gathering of medicine men for a curing ceremony but gradually coming to mean a gathering of people to celebrate an important event. In this chapter, I use the terms *Indian, American Indian,* and *indigenous people* to refer only to the indigenous people of Minnesota and western Wisconsin, unless otherwise noted. The powwow practices should be viewed as specific to the region and not necessarily generalizable beyond it. Whenever possible, I use the names of specific tribes. Nevertheless, while this chapter focuses on the powwow experiences of the Ojibwe, Dakota, Winnebago, and Menominee tribes, it is often difficult to speak in specific terms. Members of numerous tribes and bands live in Minnesota and western Wisconsin, especially in urban areas such as Minneapolis and St. Paul; and many of these people attend powwows in the area, most of which are now intertribal.

2. Some of these studies reveal more about non-Indian values than Indian problems. For example, they often fail to take account of the fact that many Indians, especially so-called fullbloods or traditionals, make a strategic and principled refusal to participate in white political and economic institutions. Moreover, some Indian people refuse to participate in BIA tribal politics because it can be viewed as condoning the BIA and, by extension, the limits to sovereignty that the BIA represents. For a poetic expression of Indian refusal

to participate in white economic institutions, see Lakota musician John Trudell's song "Wildfires" (Rykodisc 1992).

3. Seventh Annual Heart of the Earth Contest Pow Wow Program (Minneapolis, 1992), 12. See also "Heart of the Earth Survival School Celebrates 20th Anniversary," *Native American Press*, March 6, 1992. By 1991 the Red Schoolhouse had a long list of children waiting to enroll (Hamre 1991, 5).

4. Stephen Cornell uses the term *supratribal* to refer to a sense among many members of different tribes of a partly shared identity as indigenous people of North America, an identity spanning tribal differences. This emerging supratribal identity has been gradually given institutional form in organizations such as the National Congress of American Indians (NCAI), formed in the mid-1940s; the National Indian Youth Council (NIYC), formed in 1961; and the American Indian Movement (AIM) formed in Minneapolis in the late 1960s. Each of these organizations was formed in response to perceptions of shared interests and the need to address them across tribal differences. Cornell (1988, 128–38, 110) argues that urbanization primarily enabled this formation of a supratribal identity but that social activities such as the powwow also contributed. Michael A. Rynkiewich (1980, 97) lists powwows, ethnic discrimination, common (low) economic status, use of English, intertribal marriages, increasing geographical mobility, and Indian school contacts as factors contributing to a supratribal identity.

5. For example, R. D. Theisz (1987) argued that Lakota powwow songs and the powwow practices in which they are set are the centerpiece of contemporary Lakota identity formation. According to Lynn F. Huenemann (1992, 125), music and dance "are among the strongest overt expressions and measures of the perpetuation of Indian life and culture." Chris Roberts (1992, 8) argues that the powwow is the "heartbeat of Indian country" and exemplifies the "greatest renaissance [in Indian culture] since the late 1800's." Thomas W. Kavanagh (1992, 112) sees powwow music and dance as establishing an "emotional connection with the values of 'Indianness.'" Paul Robert Parthun (1976, 68) argues that "the powwow is central to the feeling of Indianess [sic]." At least some powwow participants claim to experience a "unity," a "unity of spirit," a "joining," a "unified mix of people," and a "feeling of belonging." According to the editor of a Canadian Indian magazine, *Windspeaker*, "powwows break down the barriers and unify all who take part. Whether you're from the southernmost regions of the United States or far northern Canada—common ground is found at a powwow." See David Hopkins (1991, 19) and Roberts (1992, 25, 72, 112, 9).

The following portrait of powwow experience is based on the literature on powwows and on my empirical study of powwows in Minnesota and western Wisconsin during 1988–93. My interpretation adopts the methodological approach of researchers such as Theodor W. Adorno (1932, 1948), John Miller Chernoff (1979), Helen Kivnick (1990), and Susan McClary (1991), who interpret musical practices in terms of how they model social relationships and embody ethical and political commitments.

6. For one use of this expression, see Joseph Geshick (1992, 4).

7. Most powwows include giveaways, where one or more persons will publicly give away goods or money to honor and show appreciation for the recipient(s) or some other person(s).

8. For a discussion of the philosophy and spiritualism that underlies powwow practices in Minnesota and western Minnesota, see, for example, Edward Benton-

Banai (1988). Although Benton-Banai's discussion is tied to the Ojibwe, the main themes pertinent to this chapter remain the same among tribes throughout the region.

9. Sixth Annual Heart of the Earth Contest Powwow Program (Minneapolis, 1991), 2; emcee, Lac Courte Oreilles (Wis.) Twentieth Annual Honor the Earth Homecoming Powwow, tape-recorded by the author, July 16, 1993.

10. Emcee, Lac Courte Oreilles (Wis.) Twentieth Annual Honor the Earth Homecoming Powwow, tape-recorded by the author, July 16, 1993. Children are not allowed to be carried in the dance arena because doing so represents an invitation to Mother Earth to take the child into the spirit world. Dogs used to "arrive in a cooking pot" for ceremonial dinners. Although the use of dogs in ceremonial dinners is rare today, the custom of excluding live dogs from the dance arena is sometimes still enforced. "Watching the leaders and do what they do" appeared to be an attempt to discourage inappropriate improvisation by non-Indians participating in a two-step social dance.

11. The most common songs among Minnesota and Wisconsin tribes are honor songs, veterans songs, intertribal dance songs, various contest dance songs, and forty-niner songs. For a discussion of the incomplete repetition form, see, for example, Thomas Vennum, Jr., (1989b, 8).

12. See also Reginald Laubin and Gladys Laubin (1977, 94), who argue that in powwow music "there is strength and power. . . . With several men around the drum all striking it together, all singing at the top of their lungs, the stirring, throbbing pulse of the music vibrates right through you."

13. J. S. Slotkin (1957, 14) argues that powwow drumming and singing "welds" participants "into a collective unity."

14. Tape-recorded by the author, Prairie Island, Minn., July 9, 1993.

15. For an extended discussion of this partial consolidation of styles, see, especially, William K. Powers (1990).

16. Two explanations for women's exclusion from drum groups are, first, that it is traditional and, second, that "it is strictly taboo" for a menstruating woman to participate in certain ceremonial and cultural practices (Vander 1989, 5). This form of gender inequality is not necessarily indicative of gender relations in all aspects of American Indian life. For a brief discussion of an attempt to form an all-women's drum group, see Vennum (1989a, 13). He refers to a women's drum group at Minnesota's Red Lake Ojibwe Reservation, briefly active during 1973, which was "ridiculed during their first public performance" but later met with limited, grudging acceptance. Vennum does not say how long this drum circle remained active. Finally, it should be noted that American Indian women disagree about the significance of their exclusion from drum groups. While some are critical, others defend the practice.

17. Other examples of gendered powwow practices include the fact that most emcees are male; the practice of honoring military veterans, the vast majority of whom are male; and the overall commitment to warriorism.

18. This occurred, for example, at the 1993 Lac du Flambeau (Wis.) Ojibwe powwow (John Sanford [pseud.], tape-recorded by the author, Minneapolis, June 11, 1993), the 1993 Prairie Island Dakota powwow (tape-recorded by the author, Prairie Island, Minn., July 9, 1993), and the 1991 Black River Falls Winnebago powwow (Sanford, interview, 1993).

19. Tape-recorded by the author, Minneapolis, May 20, 1993.

20. *Minneapolis Star Tribune,* May 5, 1994, p. 12E.

21. According to sales figures at the Woodland Indian Crafts Gift Shop and Craft

Store at the Minneapolis American Indian Center, a major outlet for American Indian music in the Twin Cities area, approximately 86 percent of the Indian music available in the Twin Cities in cassette or compact disc form is powwow music. Most of the rest is the crossover music of Trudell, Westerman, Harjo, Secola, and others, followed by flute and New Age music. Powwow music constitutes approximately 80 percent of actual sales, followed by crossover music at 14 percent, and flute/New Age at 6 percent.

22. Asserting the claims of one community involves, of course, a contestable assertion of a right to speak for the community. While there is strong support among Indians for treaty rights enforcement and for maintaining respect for Indian culture, Indians disagree about appropriate strategies for pursuing these goals. Some distance themselves from confrontational stances entirely and are critical of AIM in particular for its frequent use of them. In other words, while AIM faces the media as a representative of American Indians in general, it does not always enjoy the full support of the communities it is taken to represent.

23. These taunts and insults included caricatures of Indian music. For example, anti-treaty rights protesters at Big McKenzie Lake in Wisconsin on April 28, 1990, mocked the Lac du Flambeau Ojibwe singers by singing, "Hi, how are you?" and taunting the singers with statements such as "Don't you know any other words?" See the story by David Collins (1990).

24. A list of confrontational uses of powwow music would fill several pages. Drums were present, for example, at the 1972 March on Washington (the Trail of Broken Treaties); Wounded Knee, for both the 1973 takeover and the March 1993 remembrance; the march against police brutality in Minneapolis in May 1993; the Indian Religious Freedom Hearing in February 1993 in Minneapolis; the November 1992 Dakota protest against Northern States Power Company's nuclear waste storage plan; the October 1992 demonstration and protest at the U.S.-Canadian border over tobacco import taxes and other border restrictions; the November 1991 protest and demonstration over discrimination in housing and hiring practices at the office of Minneapolis mayor Donald Fraser; the July 1992 opening at Minneapolis's Uptown Theater of the film *Incident at Oglala* (the Leonard Peltier story); the mass gathering at the University of Minnesota's Northrop Auditorium to express opposition to the 1991 Gulf War; and the 1992 Inti-Illimani concert at Minneapolis's Guthrie Theatre, sponsored by the New Song Movement.

Chapter 8　*Music, Community, and Diversity*

1. Paolo Freire argues a similar point in *Pedagogy of the Oppressed* (1990). According to him, it is impossible to break the culture of silence using the methods of the oppressor.

Bibliography

Adorno, Theodor W. "The Social Situation of Music." 1932. Reprint. *Telos* 35 (spring 1978): 128–64.

———. *Introduction to the Sociology of Music.* 1962. Reprint. New York: Seabury Press, 1976.

———. *Philosophy of Modern Music.* 1948. Reprint. New York: Continuum, 1985.

Alvarez, Rodolfo, et al. "The Responsive Communitarian Platform: Rights and Responsibilities." *Responsive Community* 2 (winter 1991–92): 4–20.

Ancelet, Barry Jean. "Dewey Balfa: Cajun Music Ambassador." *Louisiana Life* (September–October 1981): 79–85.

———. *The Makers of Cajun Music.* Austin: University of Texas Press, 1984.

———. *Cajun Music: Its Origins and Development.* Lafayette: Center for Louisiana Studies, University of Southwestern Louisiana, 1989.

———. "Introduction." In *Cajun Music and Zydeco,* by Philip Gould. Baton Rouge: Louisiana State University Press, 1992a.

———. "Ragin' Cajuns: What's in a Name?" *Creole Magazine* 3 (December 1992b): 42, 44.

———. "A Tribute: Dewey Balfa, Cajun Fiddler." *Cultural Vistas* (summer 1992c): 11–17.

Ancelet, Barry Jean, Jay Edwards, and Glen Pitre. *Cajun Country.* Jackson: University Press of Mississippi, 1991.

Ancelet, Barry, and Nicholas Spitzer. Liner notes. *The Dixie Ramblers,* by Octa Clark and Hector Duhon. Somerville, Mass.: Rounder Records 6011, 1982.

Anzaldúa, Gloria. *Borderlands.* San Francisco: Spinsters/Aunt Lute, 1987.

Asante, Molefi Kete, and Kariamu Welsh Asante. *African Culture: The Rhythms of Unity.* Trenton, N.J.: Africa World Press, 1990.

Avineri, Shlomo, and Avner de-Shalit, eds. *Communitarianism and Individualism.* Oxford: Oxford University Press, 1992.

Bastien, David, and Todd Hostager. "Jazz As Social Structure, Process and Outcome." Discussion paper 77. Minneapolis: Strategic Management Research Center, University of Minnesota, July 1987.

Bell, Daniel. *Communitarianism and Its Critics.* Oxford: Clarendon Press, 1993.

Benton-Banai, Edward. *The Mishomis Book: The Voice of the Ojibway.* St. Paul: Red Schoolhouse, 1988.

Blacking, John. *How Musical Is Man?* Seattle: University of Washington Press, 1973.

Booth, Karen. "An Affair of the Heart." Lafayette (La.) *Times of Acadiana,* December 12, 1985, p. 42.

Boyte, Harry. *Commonwealth: A Return to Citizen Politics.* New York: Free Press, 1989.

———. "The Pragmatic Ends of Popular Politics." In *Habermas and the Public Sphere*, edited by Craig Calhoun. Boston: MIT Press, 1991a.

———. "Remapping Democratic Politics: Toward a Conceptualization of Public Agency." Paper presented at the presidential session on democracy, Social Science and History Association, New Orleans, November 3, 1991b.

———. "Citizenship Education and the Public World." Background paper for the civic education round table, American Political Science Association, Chicago, September 3, 1992.

Brasseaux, Carl A. *The Founding of New Acadia: The Beginning of Acadian Life in Louisiana, 1765–1803*. Baton Rouge: Louisiana State University Press, 1987.

———. *Scattered to the Wind: Dispersal and Wanderings of the Acadians, 1755–1809*. Lafayette: Center for Louisiana Studies, University of Southwestern Louisiana, 1991.

———. *Acadian to Cajun: Transformation of a People, 1803–1877*. Jackson: University Press of Mississippi, 1992.

Broven, John. *South to Louisiana: The Music of the Cajun Bayous*. Gretna, La.: Pelican Publishing, 1983.

Brunner, José Joaquín, Alicia Barrios, and Carlos Catalán. *Chile: Transformaciones culturales y modernidad*. Santiago: Facultad Latinoamericana de Ciencias Sociales (FLACSO), 1989.

Brunner, José Joaquín, and Carlos Catalán. *Industria y mercado culturales en Chile: Descripción y cuantificaciones*. Santiago: Facultad Latinoamericana de Ciencias Sociales (FLACSO), 1987.

Campbell, Horace. *Rasta and Resistance*. Trenton, N.J.: Africa World Press, 1987.

Carrasco, Eduardo. *La nueva canción en América Latina*. Santiago: Centro de Endagación y Educación Cultural y Artística (CENECA), 1982.

———. *Quilapayún: La revolución y las estrellas*. Santiago: Ediciones del Ornitorrinco, 1988.

Cary, Michael, "Political Dimensions of the Blues." *Popular Music and Society* 14 (Summer 1990): 37–48.

Chapman, John, and Ian Shapiro, eds. *Democratic Community*. New York: New York University Press, 1993.

Chavkin, Samuel. *Storm over Chile*. Chicago: Lawrence Hill Books, 1989.

Chernoff, John Miller. *African Rhythm and African Sensibility* Chicago: University of Chicago Press, 1979.

Chretien, David. "In a Diverse Culture . . . 'Cajuns' AND 'Creoles' Should Be Promoted." *Creole Magazine* 3 (November 1992): 26.

Cifuentes, Luis. *Fragmentos de un sueño: Inti-Illimani y la generación de los 60*. Santiago: Ediciones Logos, 1989.

Collins, David. "Anti-Treaty Protests in Wisconsin Lose Momentum." *Circle* 11 (May 1990): 1.

Cornell, Stephen. *The Return of the Native: American Indian Political Resurgence*. New York: Oxford University Press, 1988.

Dahl, Robert. "The Concept of Power." 1957. Reprint. In *Political Power: A Reader in Theory and Research*, edited by Roderick Bell, David M. Edwards, and R. Harrison Wagner. New York: Free Press, 1969.

Dewey, John. *Democracy and Education*. New York: Free Press, 1916.

———. *Individualism Old and New*. New York: Capricorn Books, 1930.

———. *Human Nature and Conduct*. 1922. Reprint. New York: Modern Library, 1957.

———. *Experience and Nature*. 1925. Reprint. New York: Dover Publications, 1958.

———. *Liberalism and Social Action*. 1935. Reprint. New York: Perigree Books, 1980a.

———. *The Public and Its Problems*. 1927. Reprint. Athens, Ohio: Swallow Press, 1980b.

———. *Freedom and Culture*. 1939. Reprint. Buffalo: Prometheus Books, 1989.

———. *Art As Experience*. 1934. Reprint. New York: Wideview/Perigree Books, n.d.

Digeser, Peter. "The Fourth Face of Power" *Journal of Politics* 54 (November 1992): 977–1007.

Dufilho, Arden Allen. "Beausoleil." Lafayette (La.) *Advertiser*, March 7, 1986.

———. "Jude Taylor and His Band Are Burning Up the Radio Airwaves." Lafayette (La.) *Advertiser*, January 20, 1989.

———. "Le Cajun Awards Honor Traditional Musicians." Baton Rouge *Morning Advocate*, August 13, 1990, p. 3B.

Ebbott, Elizabeth. *Indians in Minnesota*. 4th ed. Minneapolis: University of Minnesota Press, 1985.

Eidheim, Harald. "When Ethnic Identity Is a Social Stigma." In *Ethnic Groups and Boundaries: The Social Organization of Cultural Difference*, edited by Fredrik Barth. London: Allen and Unwin, 1970.

El Shabazz, Takuna Maulana. "Promotion of 'Cajun/Acadiana' Is Colonialism." *Creole Magazine* 3 (December 1992): 43, 45.

Erenberg, Lewis A. "Things to Come: Swing Bands, Bebop, and the Rise of a Postwar Jazz Scene." In *Recasting America: Culture and Politics in the Age of Cold War*, edited by Lary May. Chicago: University of Chicago Press, 1989.

Esman, Marjorie R. *Henderson, Louisiana: Cultural Adaptation in a Cajun Community*. New York: Holt, Rinehart, and Winston, 1985.

Feld, Steven. *Sound and Sentiment: Birds, Weeping, Poetics, and Song in Kaluli Expression*. Philadelphia: University of Pennsylvania Press, 1982.

Fenster, Mark. "Buck Owens, Country Music, and the Struggle for Discursive Control." *Popular Music* 9 (October 1990): 275–90.

Fish, Stanley. *Is There a Text in This Class?* Cambridge: Harvard University Press, 1980.

Fontenot, Mary Alice. "Odile Falcon Sings Songs Which Were Written More Than 400 Years Ago in French Provinces." Lafayette (La.) *Sunday Advertiser*, July 31, 1983.

Fowler, Robert Booth. *The Dance with Community: The Contemporary Debate in American Political Thought*. Lawrence: University Press of Kansas, 1991.

Freire, Paolo. *Pedagogy of the Oppressed*. New York: Continuum, 1990.

Frith, Simon. "Rock and the Politics of Memory." In *The 60s without Apology*, edited by Sohnya Sayres et al. Minneapolis: University of Minnesota Press, 1984.

———, ed. *World Music, Politics and Social Change*. Manchester, England: Manchester University Press, 1989.

Fry, Macon, and Julie Posner. *Cajun Country Guide*. Gretna, La.: Pelican Publishing, 1992.

García, Ricardo. Untitled. In *La producción de música popular en Chile*, edited by Valerio Fuenzalida. Santiago: Centro de Endagación y Educación Cultural y Artística (CENECA), 1987.

Gaventa, John. *Power and Powerlessness*. Urbana: University of Chicago Press, 1980.

Geshick, Joseph. Letter to the editor. *Native American Press*, July 17, 1992, p. 4.

Gilfoil, Buffy. "'Chantez encore': New Book Features Cajun Folk Songs." Baton Rouge *Morning Advocate*, October 24, 1977.

Gilmore, Robert, and Jeanne Gilmore. *Chantez, la Louisiane! Louisiana French Folk Songs*. Lafayette, La: Acadiana Music, 1970.

————. *Chantez encore: Folksongs of French South Louisiana*. Gretna, La.: Pelican Publishing, 1977.

Gilroy, Paul. *There Ain't No Black in the Union Jack*. London: Hutchinson, 1987.

Gitlin, Todd. *The Twilight of Common Dreams: Why America Is Wracked by Culture Wars*. New York: Metropolitan Books, 1995.

Godoy, Alvaro. *La bicicleta: Éste especial* [A special edition of the magazine *La Bicicleta* devoted to canto nuevo]. Santiago: Editora Granizo, 1981.

Gould, Philip. *Cajun Music and Zydeco*. Baton Rouge: Louisiana State University Press, 1992.

Gramsci, Antonio. *Selections from the Prison Notebooks*, edited by Quintin Hoare and Geoffrey Nowell Smith. New York: International Publishers, 1971.

————. *Selections from Cultural Writings*, edited by David Forgacs and Geoffrey Nowell Smith. Cambridge: Harvard University Press, 1985.

Greenway, John. *American Folksongs of Protest*. New York: Octagon Books, 1977.

Grindstaff, Burton. Editorial. Opelousas (La.) *Daily World*, October 20, 1965.

Grossberg, Lawrence. "Another Boring Day in Paradise: Rock and Roll and the Empowerment of Everyday Life." *Popular Music* 4 (1984): 225–58.

Guillory, Wilbert, Liz Savoy, and Paul Scott. Brochure for the Original Southwest Louisiana Zydeco Music Festival. Plaisance, La., 1993.

Hamre, Susan. "Red Schoolhouse Gives Indians Necessary Alternatives." *Native American Press*, October 25, 1991, p. 5.

Hannusch, Jeff. Liner notes. *Turning Point*, by Buckwheat Zydeco and the Ils Sont Partis Band. Somerville, Mass.: Rounder Records 2045, 1983.

"Heart of the Earth Survival School Celebrates 20th Anniversary." *Native American Press*, March 6, 1992, p. 1.

Hebdige, Dick. *Cut-n-Mix: Culture, Identity, and Caribbean Music*. London: Methuen, 1987.

Heth, Charlotte, ed. *Native American Dance: Ceremonies and Social Traditions*. Washington, D.C.: National Museum of the American Indian, Smithsonian Institution, with Starwood Publishing, 1992.

Hirsch, H. N. "The Threnody of Liberalism: Constitutional Liberty and the Renewal of Community." *Political Theory* 14, no. 3 (1986): 423–49.

Hopkins, David. "Truly an Explosion of Culture." *Circle* 12 (October 1991): 19.

Huenemann, Lynn F. "Northern Plains Dance." In *Native American Dance: Ceremonies and Social Traditions*, edited by Charlotte Heth. Washington, D.C.: National Museum of the American Indian, Smithsonian Institution, with Starwood Publishing, 1992.

Huggs, Katrinna. "Musical Geniuses and Friends." Lafayette (La.) *Times of Acadiana*, September 22, 1993, p. 11.

Hylton, Patrick. "The Politics of Caribbean Music." *Black Scholar* 7 (September 1975): 23–29.

James, David. "The Vietnam War and American Music." *Social Text* 8 (fall–winter 1989): 122–43.

Jara, Joan. *Victor Jara: Un canto no truncado*. Santiago: Literatura Americana Reunida, 1988.

Jones, LeRoi. *Blues People*. New York: William Morrow, 1963.

Kavanagh, Thomas W. "Southern Plains Dance: Tradition and Dynamism." In *Native American Dance: Ceremonies and Social Traditions*, edited by Charlotte Heth. Washington, D.C.: National Museum of the American Indian, Smithsonian Institution, with Starwood Publishing, 1992.

Kedinger, Paul. "Grammy Nominees Commended for Musical Heritage." *Ville Platte (La.) Gazette*, April 7, 1986.

Keil, Charles. *TIV Song: The Sociology of Art in a Classless Society*. Chicago: University of Chicago Press, 1979.

King, Martin Luther, Jr. *I Have a Dream: Writings and Speeches That Changed the World*, edited by James M. Washington. New York: HarperCollins Publishers, 1992.

Kivnick, Helen. *Where Is the Way: Song and Struggle in South Africa*. New York: Penguin Books, 1990.

Krader, Barbara. "Slavic Folk Music: Forms of Singing and Self-Identity." *Ethnomusicology* 31 (Winter 1987): 9–17.

Largo Farías, René, ed. *Revista de Folklore* 1, no. 1 (1970).

———. *Cuadernos de Casa de Chile, no. 9*. Mexico City: Casa de Chile, 1977.

Laubin, Reginald, and Gladys Laubin. *Indian Dances of North America*. Norman: University of Oklahoma Press, 1977.

Leland, John. "Rap and Race." *Newsweek*, June 29, 1992, pp. 46–52.

Leppert, Richard, and Susan McClary. *Music and Society: The Politics of Composition, Performance, and Reception*. Cambridge: Cambridge University Press, 1987.

Lewis, George. "Storm Blowing from Paradise: Social Protest and Oppositional Ideology in Popular Hawaiian Music." *Popular Music* 10 (January 1991): 53–67.

Lipsitz, George. *Time Passages: Collective Memory and American Popular Culture*. Minneapolis: University of Minnesota Press, 1990.

Loveman, Brian. "Antipolitics in Chile, 1973–94." In *The Politics of Antipolitics*, edited by Brian Loveman and Thomas Davies. Wilmington, Del.: Scholarly Resources.

Luther, Martin. Preface. In *Symphoniae jucundae*. 1538. Reprint. In *Luther's Works*, vol. 53, translated by Ulrich S. Leupold. Philadelphia: Fortress Press, 1965.

Manuel, Peter. "Andalusian, Gypsy, and Class Identity in the Contemporary Flamenco Complex." *Ethnomusicology* 33 (Winter 1989): 47–65.

Marcus, George E., and Michael M. J. Fischer. *Anthropology As Cultural Critique*. Chicago: University of Chicago Press, 1986.

McClary, Susan. *Feminine Endings: Music, Gender and Sexuality*. Minneapolis: University of Minnesota Press, 1991.

McConnaughey, Janet. "Mouton's Accordions 'Shine.'" *Lafayette (La.) Advertiser*, June 11, 1990.

Mella, Luis, Carlos Catalán, Anny Rivera, and Rodrigo Torres. *Seminario: La canción popular chilena (1973–1979)*. Santiago: Centro de Endagación y Educación Cultural y Artística (CENECA), 1980.

Mills, Lynn. "Music Is Everything for Acadiana Zydeco Performer." *Lafayette (La.) Sunday Advertiser*, October 24, 1982, p. 25E.

Minneapolis Star Tribune. May 5, 1994, p. 12F.

Mondak, Jeffery. "Protest Music As Political Persuasion." *Popular Music and Society* 12 (Fall 1988): 25–38.

Mouffe, Chantal. "Democratic Citizenship and the Political Community." In *Community at Loose Ends*, edited by the Miami Theory Collective. Minneapolis: University of Minnesota Press, 1991.

Parthun, Paul Robert. "Ojibwe Music in Minnesota." Ph.D. diss., University of Minnesota, 1976.

Patterson, Tim. "Notes on the Historical Application of Marxist Cultural Theory." *Science and Society* 39 (fall 1975): 257–91.

Peña, Manuel. *The Texas-Mexican Conjunto: History of a Working Class Music*. Austin: University of Texas Press, 1985.

Plato. *The Republic*. **correct?**]] Reprint. Indianapolis: Hackett Publishing, 1974, para. 424c.

Powers, William K. *War Dance: Plains Indian Musical Performance*. Tucson: University of Arizona Press, 1990.

Pratt, Ray. "Popular Music, Free Space, and the Quest for Community." *Popular Music and Society* 13 (winter 1989): 59–76.

———. *Rhythm and Resistance: Explorations in the Political Uses of Popular Music*. New York: Praeger, 1990.

Ramet, Sabrina Petra. *Rocking the State: Rock Music and Politics in Eastern Europe and Russia*. Boulder: Westview Press, 1994.

Reagon, Bernice Johnson, "The Power of Communal Song." In *Cultures in Contention*, edited by Douglas Kahn and Diane Neumaier. Seattle: Real Comet Press, 1985.

Reyes Matta, Fernando. "The 'New Song' and Its Confrontation in Latin America." In *Marxism and the Interpretation of Culture*, edited by Cary Nelson and Lawrence Grossberg. Urbana: University of Illinois Press, 1988.

Rivera, Anny. *El público del canto popular*. Santiago: Centro de Endagación y Educación Cultural y Artística (CENECA), 1980.

———. *Notas sobre movimiento social y arte en el régimen autoritario*. Santiago: Centro de Endagación y Educación Cultural y Artística (CENECA), 1983.

———. *Transformaciones de la industria músical en Chile*. Santiago: Centro de Endagación y Educación Cultural y Artística (CENECA), 1984.

Rivera, Anny, and Rodrigo Torres. *Encuentro de canto poblacional*.Santiago: Centro de Endagación y Educación Cultural y Artística (CENECA), 1981.

Roberts, Chris. *Powwow Country*. Helena, Mont.: American and World Geographic Publishing, 1992.

Rodnitzky, Jerome L. *Minstrels of the Dawn: The Folk-Protest Singer As a Cultural Hero*. Chicago: Nelson-Hall, 1976.

Rosaldo, Renato. "Ideology, Place, and People without Culture." *Cultural Anthropology* 3 (February 1988): 77–87.

Rose, Tricia. *Black Noise: Rap Music and Black Culture in Contemporary America*. Hanover, N.H.: Wesleyan University Press, 1994.

Rynkiewich, Michael A. "Chippewa Powwows." In *Anishinabe: 6 Studies of Modern Chippewa*, edited by J. Anthony Paredes. Tallahassee: University Presses of Florida, 1980.

Sandmel, Ben. "Bon Temps on the Air." *Louisiana Life* 12 (April–May 1992): 61–63.

———. Liner notes. *Parlez-nous à boire*, by Michael Doucet with Beausoleil. Berkeley, Calif.: Arhoolie Records 5034, 1984.

Savoy, Ann A. *Cajun Music: A Reflection of a People*. Vol. 1. Eunice, La.: Bluebird Press, 1984.

Schlesinger, Arthur M., Jr. *The Disuniting of America: Reflections on a Multicultural Society*. New York: W. W. Norton, 1991.

Setti, Kilza. "Notes on Caicara Musical Production: Music As the Focus of Cultural Resistance among the Fisherman of the Coastal Region of São Paulo." *World of Music: Bulletin of the International Music Council* 30, no. 3 (1988): 3–21.

Seventh Annual Heart of the Earth Survival School Contest Powwow. Program. Minneapolis Convention Center, March 27–29, 1992.

Shelton, Melinda. "State Musician Keeps Cajun Sound Alive." Baton Rouge *Sunday Advocate*, March 2, 1982, pp. 8, 8D.

Simon, Dixie. "Zachary Richard Comes Home to Scott." Lafayette (La.) *Advertiser*, February 14, 1993, p. A13.

Simoneaux, Angela. "Growth, not Change, Is Seen As Key to Preserving Traditional Cajun Music." Baton Rouge *Sunday Advocate*, March 22, 1992, pp. 1B, 5B.

Sixth Annual Heart of the Earth Contest Powwow. Program. Minneapolis Convention Center, February 22–24, 1991.

Slotkin, J. S. *The Menomini Powwow*. Milwaukee: Milwaukee Public Museum, 1957.

Small, Christopher. *Music of the Common Tongue: Survival and Celebration in Afro-American Music*. London: John Calder Publishers, 1987.

Spencer, Jon Michael, ed. *The Emergency of Black and the Emergence of Rap*. Durham: Duke University Press, 1991.

Spitzer, Nicholas. Liner notes. *The Dixie Ramblers—Ensemble encore*, by Octa Clark and Hector Duhon. Somerville, Mass.: Rounder Records 6011, 1982.

Stanford, Ron, and Fay Stanford. Booklet. *J'étais au bal: Music from French Louisiana*. Ville Platte, La.: Swallow Records 6020, 1974.

Theisz, R. D. "Song Texts and Their Performers: The Centerpiece of Contemporary Lakota Identity Formulation." *Great Plains Quarterly* 7 (Spring 1987): 116–24.

Tillson, Becky. "Guidry out to Preserve the Cajun Sound." Lafayette (La.) *Advertiser*, January 24, 1993.

Valenzuela, J. Samuel, and Arturo Valenzuela. "Chile and the Breakdown of Democracy." In *Latin American Politics and Development*, edited by Howard Wiarda and Harvey Kline. Boulder: Westview Press, 1985.

Vander, Judith. "From the Musical Experience of Five Shoshone Women." In *Women in North American Indian Music*, edited by Richard Keeling. Bloomington, Ind.: Society for Ethnomusicology, Special Series, no. 6, 1989.

Vennum, Thomas, Jr. *The Ojibwa Dance Drum: Its History and Construction*. Washington, D.C.: Smithsonian Institute Press, 1982.

———. "The Changing Role of Women in Ojibway Music History." In *Women in North American Indian Music*, edited by Richard Keeling. Society for Ethnomusicology, Special Series, no. 6, 1989a.

———. *Ojibway Music from Minnesota: Continuity and Change*. St. Paul: Minnesota Historical Society Press and the Minnesota State Arts Board, 1989b.

Walser, Rob. *Running with the Devil: Power, Gender and Madness in Heavy Metal Music*. Hanover, N.H.: Wesleyan University Press, 1993.

Wartenberg, Thomas. *The Forms of Power*. Philadelphia: Temple University Press, 1990.

Watters, Pat. "Different Worlds." Lafayette (La.) *Times*, September 29, 1993, pp. 12–22. Reprinted as "Talking about Race in Lafayette." *Nation*, November 22, 1993, 611–14.

Williams, Raymond. *The Long Revolution*. (London: Cox and Wyman, 1961.

Winthrop, John. "A Modell of Christian Charity" 1630. Reprint. In *American Political Thinking*, edited by Robert Isaak. Fort Worth, Tex.: Harcourt Brace College Publishers, 1994.

Young, Iris. "The Ideal of Community and the Politics of Difference." In *Feminism/Postmodernism*, edited by Linda Nicholson. New York: Routledge, 1990.

Index

About the Author

Mark Mattern is assistant professor of political science at Chapman University in Orange, California. He teaches courses in political theory, popular culture, and political economy.